MW01283526

THIS JOURNAL BELONGS TO:

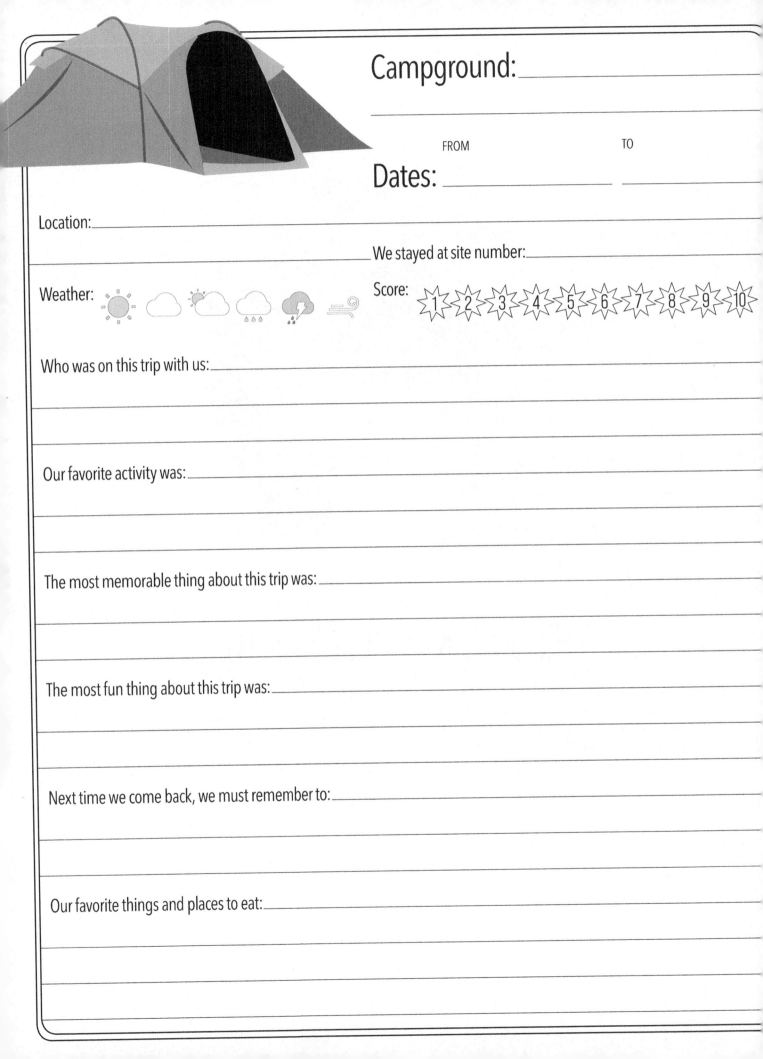

Campground: _____

_____

FROM   TO

Dates: _____ _____

Location: _____

We stayed at site number: _____

Weather:

Score: 1 2 3 4 5 6 7 8 9 10

Who was on this trip with us: _____

Our favorite activity was: _____

The most memorable thing about this trip was: _____

The most fun thing about this trip was: _____

Next time we come back, we must remember to: _____

Our favorite things and places to eat: _____

Other Notes:_____

A drawing or photo of the favorite part of our stay:

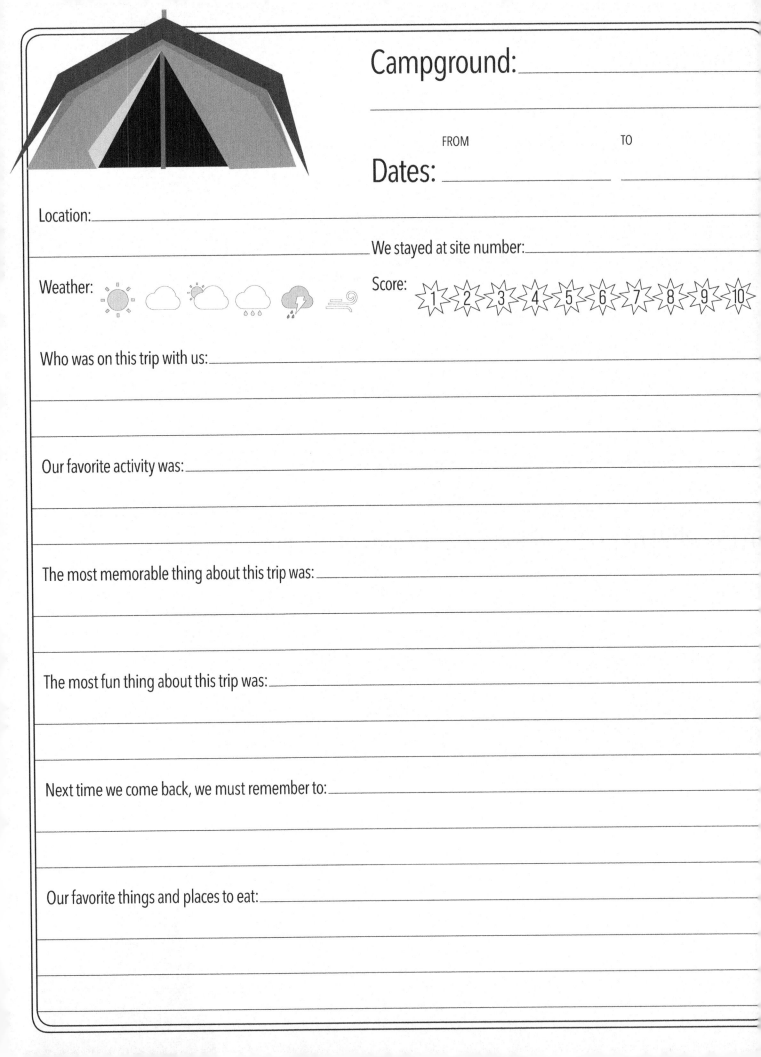

Campground: _____

_____

FROM   TO

Dates: _____   _____

Location: _____

We stayed at site number: _____

Weather: ☀ ☁ ⛅ 🌧 ⛈ 🌬   Score: 1 2 3 4 5 6 7 8 9 10

Who was on this trip with us: _____

_____

_____

Our favorite activity was: _____

_____

_____

The most memorable thing about this trip was: _____

_____

_____

The most fun thing about this trip was: _____

_____

_____

Next time we come back, we must remember to: _____

_____

_____

Our favorite things and places to eat: _____

_____

_____

Other Notes:

A drawing or photo of the favorite part of our stay:

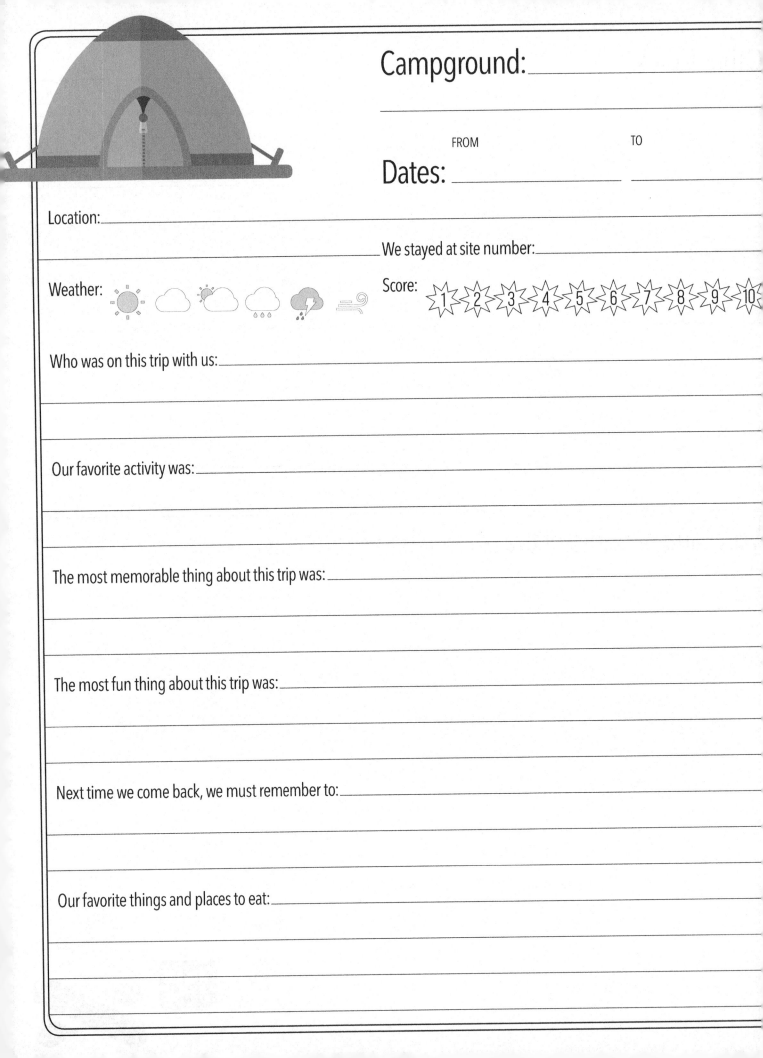

Campground: _____

_____

FROM   TO

Dates: _____ _____

Location: _____

We stayed at site number: _____

Weather: ☀ ☁ ⛅ 🌧 ⛈ 🌬   Score: 1 2 3 4 5 6 7 8 9 10

Who was on this trip with us: _____

_____

_____

Our favorite activity was: _____

_____

_____

The most memorable thing about this trip was: _____

_____

_____

The most fun thing about this trip was: _____

_____

_____

Next time we come back, we must remember to: _____

_____

_____

Our favorite things and places to eat: _____

_____

_____

_____

Other Notes:

A drawing or photo of the favorite part of our stay:

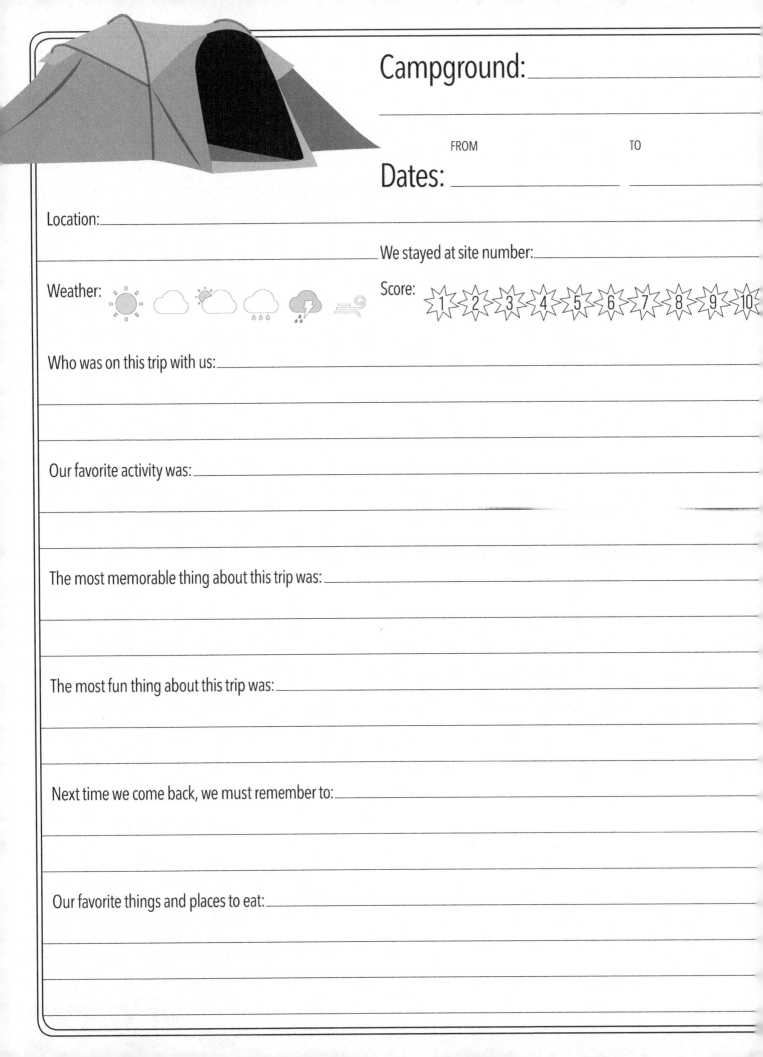

Campground: _____

_____

FROM   TO

Dates: _____   _____

Location: _____

_____ We stayed at site number: _____

Weather: Score: 1 2 3 4 5 6 7 8 9 10

Who was on this trip with us: _____

_____

_____

Our favorite activity was: _____

_____

_____

The most memorable thing about this trip was: _____

_____

_____

The most fun thing about this trip was: _____

_____

_____

Next time we come back, we must remember to: _____

_____

_____

Our favorite things and places to eat: _____

_____

_____

Other Notes:_____

_____

_____

_____

_____

_____

_____

_____

_____

_____

_____

_____

A drawing or photo of the favorite part of our stay:

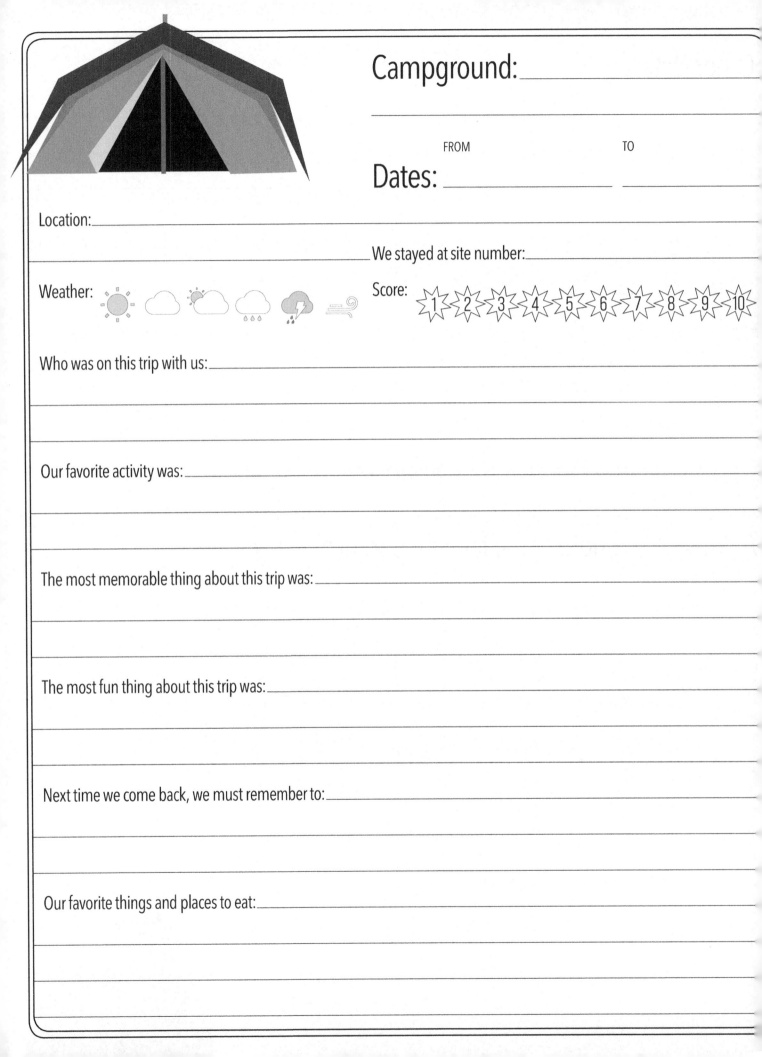

Campground: _____

_____

FROM _____ TO _____

Dates: _____ _____

Location: _____

We stayed at site number: _____

Weather: ☀ ☁ ⛅ 🌧 ⛈ 🌬

Score: 1 2 3 4 5 6 7 8 9 10

Who was on this trip with us: _____

_____

_____

Our favorite activity was: _____

_____

_____

The most memorable thing about this trip was: _____

_____

_____

The most fun thing about this trip was: _____

_____

_____

Next time we come back, we must remember to: _____

_____

_____

Our favorite things and places to eat: _____

_____

_____

Other Notes:

A drawing or photo of the favorite part of our stay:

Campground: _____

_____

Dates: _____   _____
FROM   TO

Location: _____

_____ We stayed at site number: _____

Weather: ☀ ☁ ⛅ ☁ ⛈ 🌬   Score: 1 2 3 4 5 6 7 8 9 10

Who was on this trip with us: _____

_____

_____

_____

Our favorite activity was: _____

_____

_____

_____

The most memorable thing about this trip was: _____

_____

_____

_____

The most fun thing about this trip was: _____

_____

_____

_____

Next time we come back, we must remember to: _____

_____

_____

_____

Our favorite things and places to eat: _____

_____

_____

_____

Other Notes:

A drawing or photo of the favorite part of our stay:

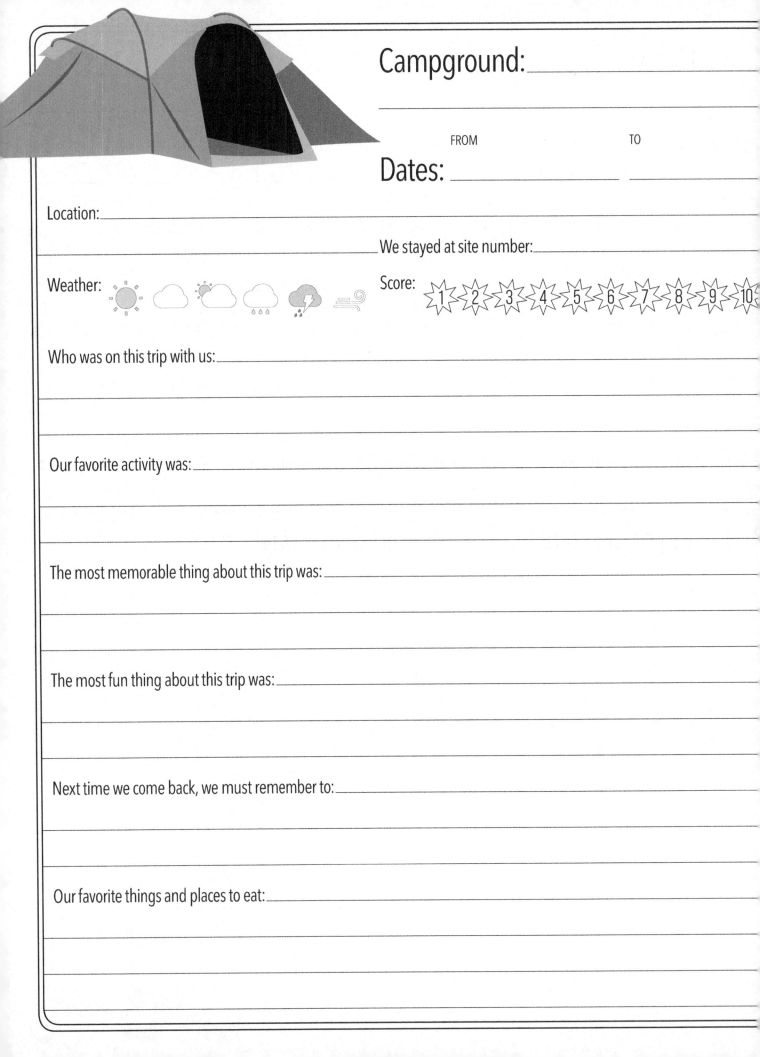

Campground:_____

_____

FROM   TO

Dates: _____ _____

Location:_____

_____ We stayed at site number:_____

Weather: ☀   ☁   ⛅   🌧   ⛈   🌬   Score: ☆1☆2☆3☆4☆5☆6☆7☆8☆9☆10

Who was on this trip with us:_____

_____

_____

Our favorite activity was:_____

_____

_____

The most memorable thing about this trip was:_____

_____

_____

The most fun thing about this trip was:_____

_____

_____

Next time we come back, we must remember to:_____

_____

_____

Our favorite things and places to eat:_____

_____

_____

Other Notes:

_____

_____

_____

_____

_____

_____

_____

_____

_____

_____

A drawing or photo of the favorite part of our stay:

Campground: _____

_____

FROM   TO

Dates: _____ _____

Location: _____

We stayed at site number: _____

Weather: ☀ ☁ ⛅ 🌧 ⛈ 🌬   Score: 1 2 3 4 5 6 7 8 9 10

Who was on this trip with us: _____

_____

_____

Our favorite activity was: _____

_____

_____

The most memorable thing about this trip was: _____

_____

_____

The most fun thing about this trip was: _____

_____

_____

Next time we come back, we must remember to: _____

_____

_____

Our favorite things and places to eat: _____

_____

_____

_____

Other Notes: _____
_____
_____
_____
_____
_____
_____
_____
_____
_____
_____

A drawing or photo of the favorite part of our stay:

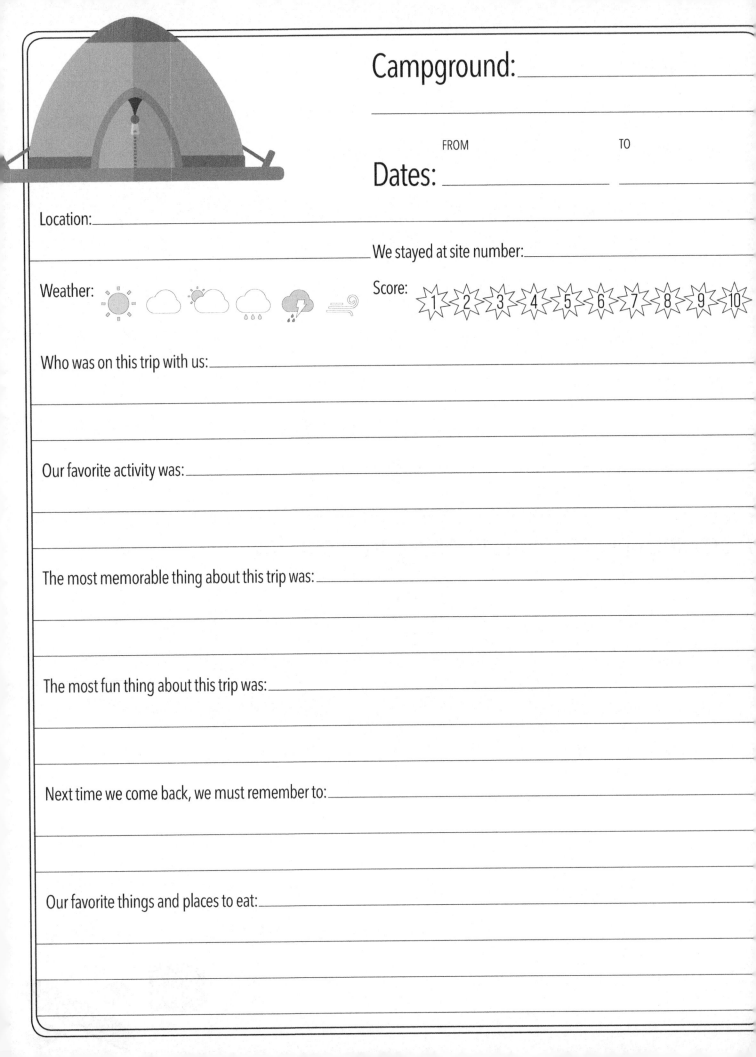

Campground: _____

_____

FROM   TO
Dates: _____   _____

Location: _____

_____ We stayed at site number: _____

Weather: ☀ ☁ ⛅ 🌧 ⛈ 🌬   Score: 1 2 3 4 5 6 7 8 9 10

Who was on this trip with us: _____

_____

_____

Our favorite activity was: _____

_____

_____

The most memorable thing about this trip was: _____

_____

_____

The most fun thing about this trip was: _____

_____

_____

Next time we come back, we must remember to: _____

_____

_____

Our favorite things and places to eat: _____

_____

_____

_____

Other Notes:

A drawing or photo of the favorite part of our stay:

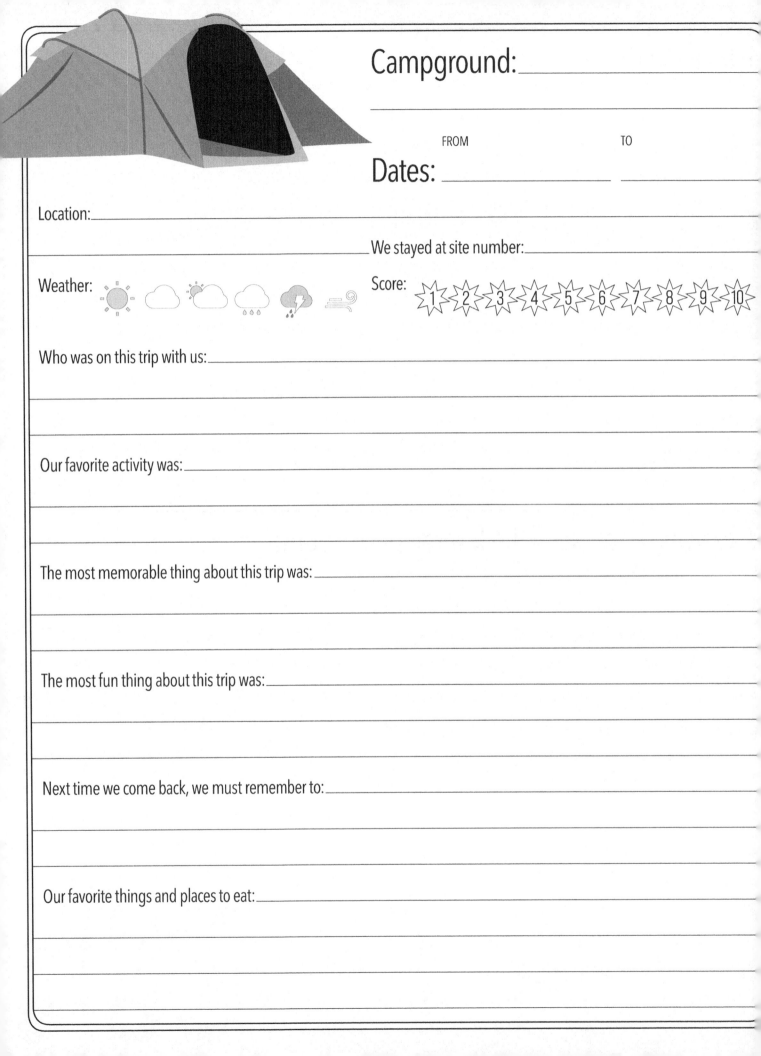

Campground: _____

_____

FROM   TO

Dates: _____ _____

Location: _____

_____ We stayed at site number: _____

Weather: ☀ ☁ ⛅ 🌧 ⛈ 🌬   Score: 1 2 3 4 5 6 7 8 9 10

Who was on this trip with us: _____

_____

_____

Our favorite activity was: _____

_____

_____

The most memorable thing about this trip was: _____

_____

_____

The most fun thing about this trip was: _____

_____

_____

Next time we come back, we must remember to: _____

_____

_____

Our favorite things and places to eat: _____

_____

_____

Other Notes:

A drawing or photo of the favorite part of our stay:

Campground: _____

_____

FROM   TO

Dates: _____   _____

Location: _____

_____

We stayed at site number: _____

Weather:

Score: 1 2 3 4 5 6 7 8 9 10

Who was on this trip with us: _____

_____

_____

Our favorite activity was: _____

_____

_____

The most memorable thing about this trip was: _____

_____

_____

The most fun thing about this trip was: _____

_____

_____

Next time we come back, we must remember to: _____

_____

_____

Our favorite things and places to eat: _____

_____

_____

_____

Other Notes:_____

_____

_____

_____

_____

_____

_____

_____

_____

_____

_____

_____

A drawing or photo of the favorite part of our stay:

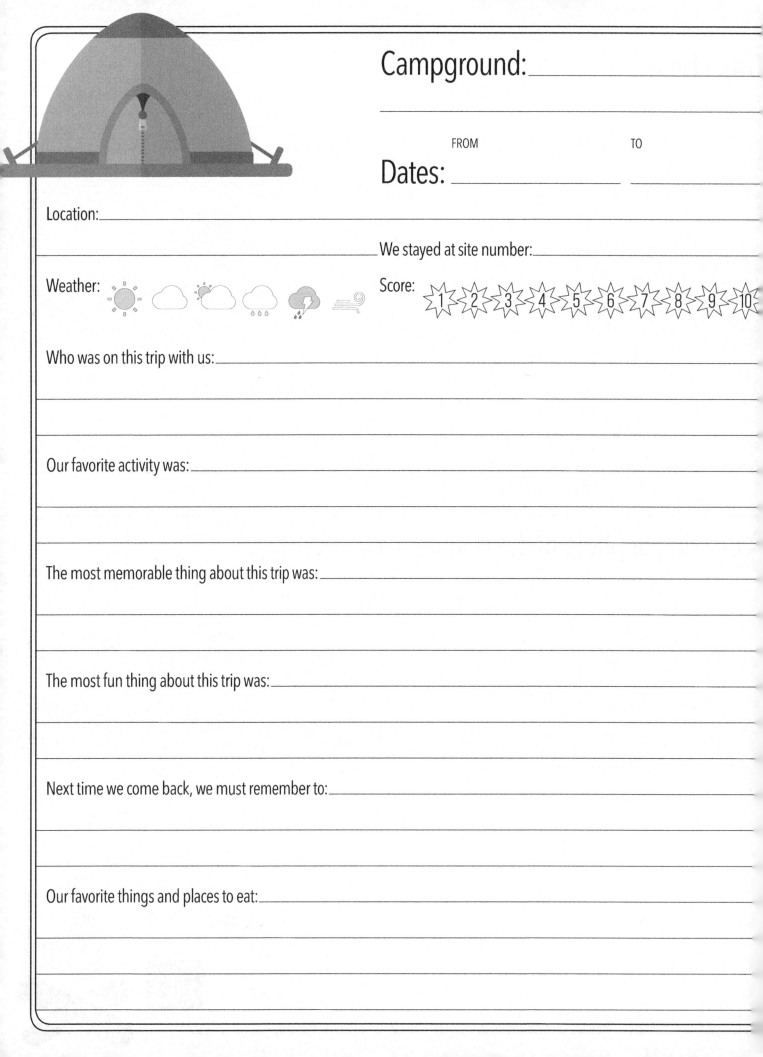

Campground:

FROM   TO

Dates:

Location:

We stayed at site number:

Weather:

Score: 1 2 3 4 5 6 7 8 9 10

Who was on this trip with us:

Our favorite activity was:

The most memorable thing about this trip was:

The most fun thing about this trip was:

Next time we come back, we must remember to:

Our favorite things and places to eat:

Other Notes:_____

_____

_____

_____

_____

_____

_____

_____

_____

_____

A drawing or photo of the favorite part of our stay:

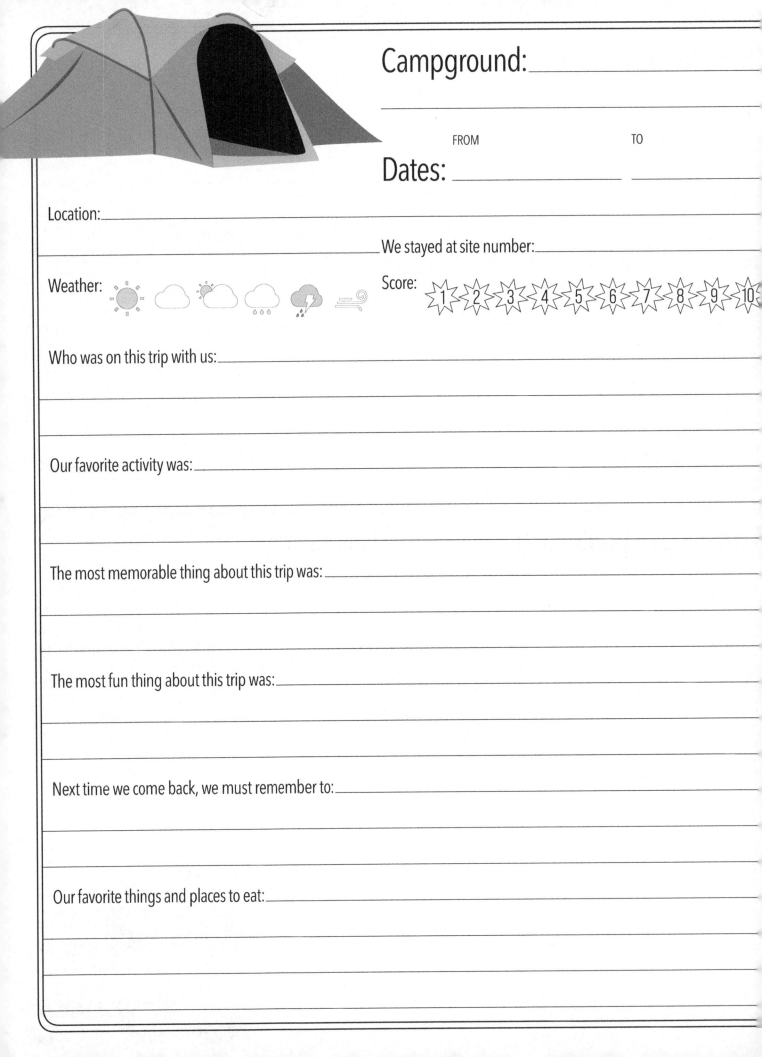

Campground: _____

_____

FROM   TO

Dates: _____   _____

Location: _____

_____ We stayed at site number: _____

Weather: ☀ ☁ ⛅ 🌧 ⛈ 🌬   Score: 1 2 3 4 5 6 7 8 9 10

Who was on this trip with us: _____

_____

_____

Our favorite activity was: _____

_____

_____

The most memorable thing about this trip was: _____

_____

_____

The most fun thing about this trip was: _____

_____

_____

Next time we come back, we must remember to: _____

_____

_____

Our favorite things and places to eat: _____

_____

_____

Other Notes:
_____

_____

_____

_____

_____

_____

_____

_____

_____

_____

_____

A drawing or photo of the favorite part of our stay:

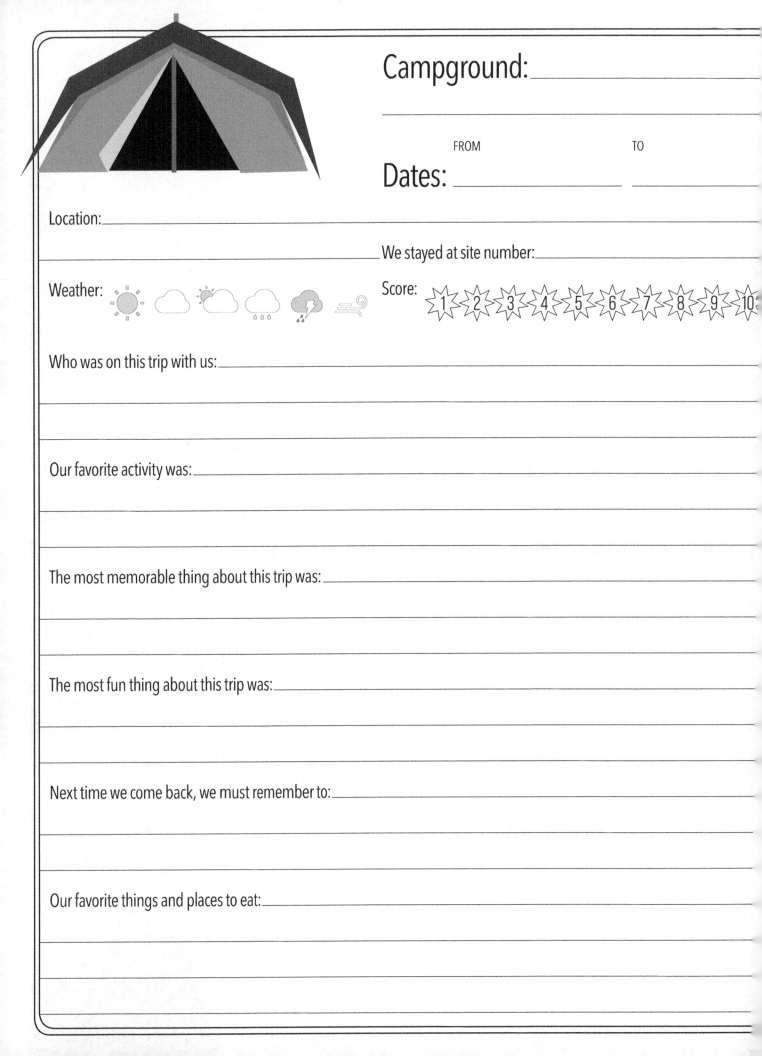

Campground: _____

_____

FROM   TO

Dates: _____   _____

Location: _____

_____ We stayed at site number: _____

Weather:

Score: 1 2 3 4 5 6 7 8 9 10

Who was on this trip with us: _____

_____

_____

Our favorite activity was: _____

_____

_____

The most memorable thing about this trip was: _____

_____

_____

The most fun thing about this trip was: _____

_____

_____

Next time we come back, we must remember to: _____

_____

_____

Our favorite things and places to eat: _____

_____

_____

_____

Other Notes:_____

A drawing or photo of the favorite part of our stay:

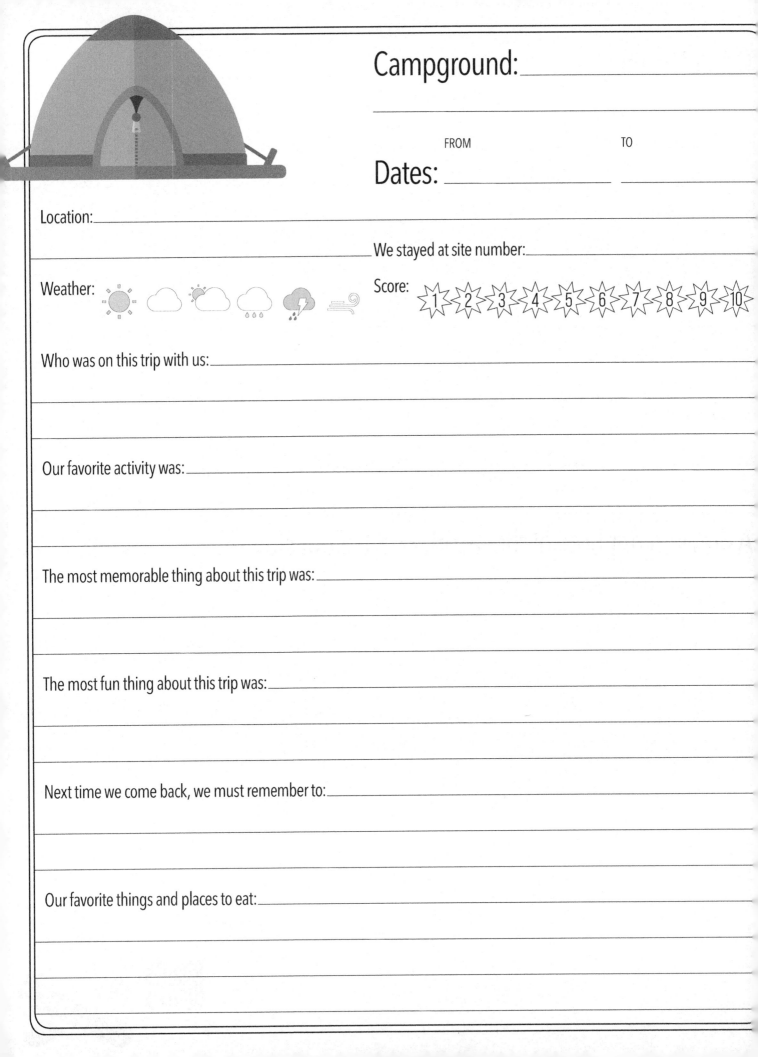

Campground: _____

_____

FROM   TO

Dates: _____   _____

Location: _____

We stayed at site number: _____

Weather: Score: 1 2 3 4 5 6 7 8 9 10

Who was on this trip with us: _____

Our favorite activity was: _____

The most memorable thing about this trip was: _____

The most fun thing about this trip was: _____

Next time we come back, we must remember to: _____

Our favorite things and places to eat: _____

Other Notes:

A drawing or photo of the favorite part of our stay:

Campground: _____
_____

FROM _____ TO _____

Dates: _____

Location: _____
_____

We stayed at site number: _____

Weather: ☀ ☁ ⛅ 🌧 ⛈ 🌬

Score: 1 2 3 4 5 6 7 8 9 10

Who was on this trip with us: _____
_____
_____
_____

Our favorite activity was: _____
_____
_____

The most memorable thing about this trip was: _____
_____
_____

The most fun thing about this trip was: _____
_____
_____

Next time we come back, we must remember to: _____
_____
_____

Our favorite things and places to eat: _____
_____
_____
_____

Other Notes:_____

A drawing or photo of the favorite part of our stay:

Campground: _____

_____

FROM   TO

Dates: _____   _____

Location: _____

_____ We stayed at site number: _____

Weather: Score: 1 2 3 4 5 6 7 8 9 10

Who was on this trip with us: _____

_____

_____

Our favorite activity was: _____

_____

_____

The most memorable thing about this trip was: _____

_____

_____

The most fun thing about this trip was: _____

_____

_____

Next time we come back, we must remember to: _____

_____

_____

Our favorite things and places to eat: _____

_____

_____

_____

Other Notes:_____

A drawing or photo of the favorite part of our stay:

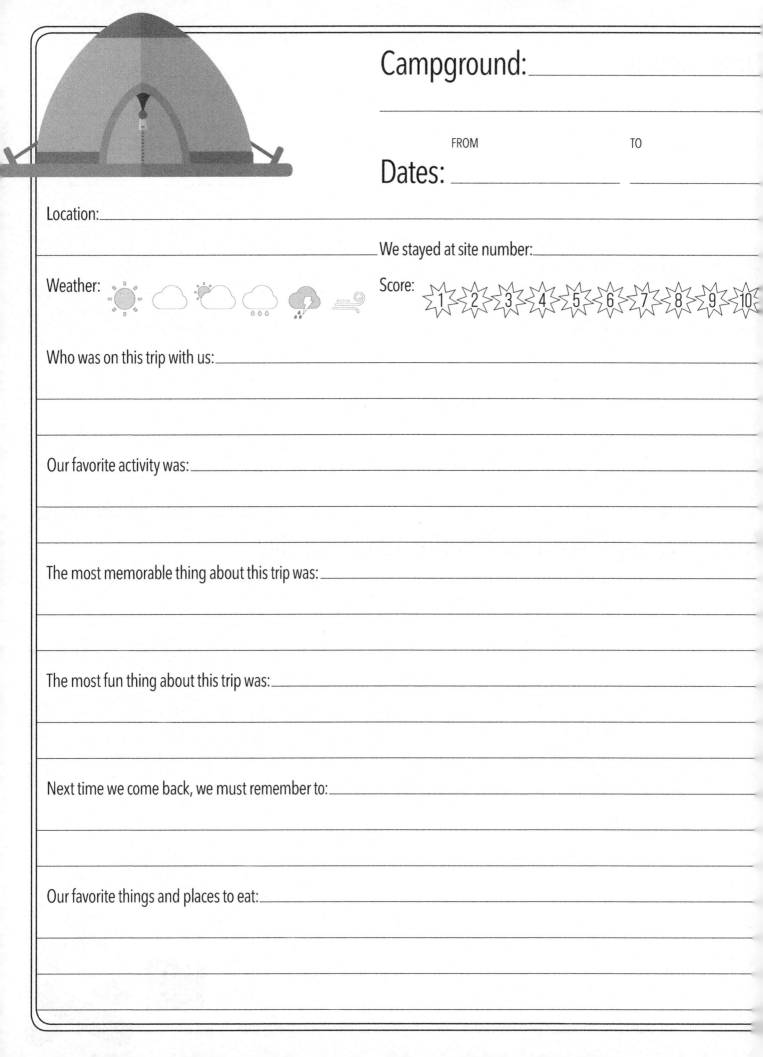

Campground: _____

_____

FROM _____ TO _____

Dates: _____ _____

Location: _____

_____ We stayed at site number: _____

Weather: Score: 1 2 3 4 5 6 7 8 9 10

Who was on this trip with us: _____

_____

_____

Our favorite activity was: _____

_____

_____

The most memorable thing about this trip was: _____

_____

_____

The most fun thing about this trip was: _____

_____

_____

_____

Next time we come back, we must remember to: _____

_____

_____

Our favorite things and places to eat: _____

_____

_____

_____

Other Notes:

A drawing or photo of the favorite part of our stay:

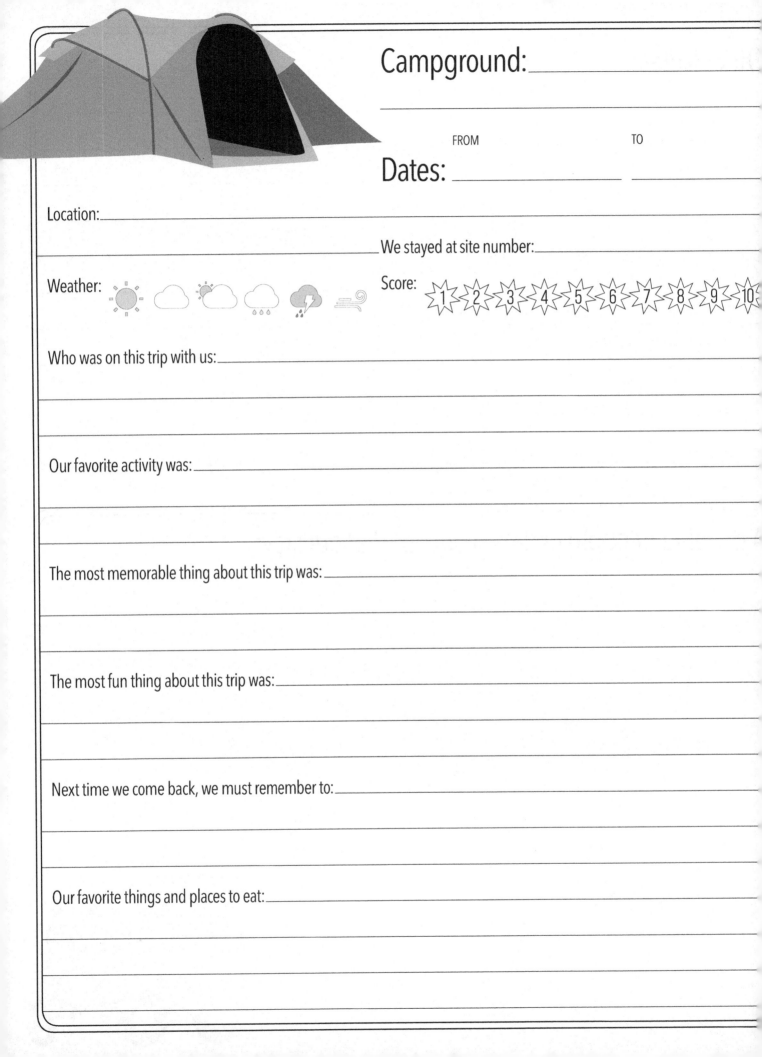

Campground:_____

_____

FROM   TO

Dates: _____   _____

Location:_____

_____ We stayed at site number:_____

Weather: ☀ ☁ ⛅ 🌧 ⛈ 🌬   Score: ⟨1⟩⟨2⟩⟨3⟩⟨4⟩⟨5⟩⟨6⟩⟨7⟩⟨8⟩⟨9⟩⟨10⟩

Who was on this trip with us:_____

_____

_____

Our favorite activity was:_____

_____

_____

The most memorable thing about this trip was:_____

_____

_____

The most fun thing about this trip was:_____

_____

_____

Next time we come back, we must remember to:_____

_____

_____

Our favorite things and places to eat:_____

_____

_____

Other Notes:
_____

_____

_____

_____

_____

_____

_____

_____

_____

_____

_____

_____

A drawing or photo of the favorite part of our stay:

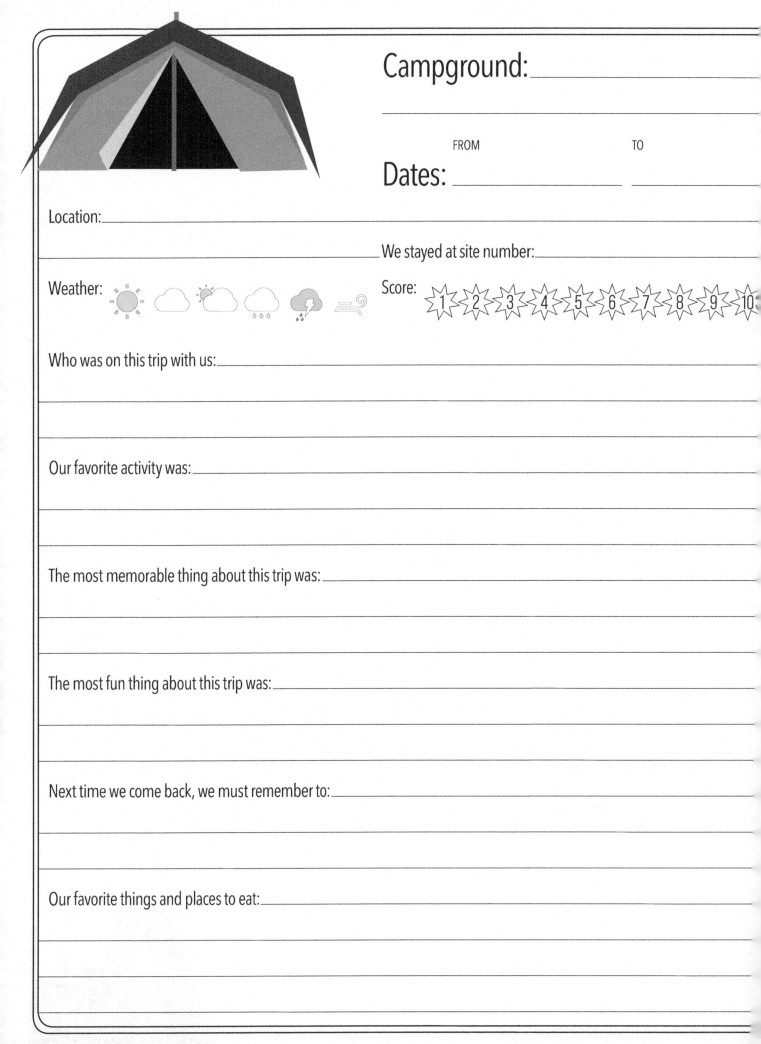

Campground: _____

_____

FROM   TO
Dates: _____   _____

Location: _____

_____ We stayed at site number: _____

Weather: Score: 1 2 3 4 5 6 7 8 9 10

Who was on this trip with us: _____

_____

_____

Our favorite activity was: _____

_____

_____

The most memorable thing about this trip was: _____

_____

_____

The most fun thing about this trip was: _____

_____

_____

Next time we come back, we must remember to: _____

_____

_____

Our favorite things and places to eat: _____

_____

_____

_____

Other Notes:

A drawing or photo of the favorite part of our stay:

Campground: _____

_____

FROM   TO

Dates: _____ _____

Location: _____

We stayed at site number: _____

Weather: ☀ ☁ ⛅ 🌧 ⛈ 💨   Score: 1 2 3 4 5 6 7 8 9 10

Who was on this trip with us: _____

_____

Our favorite activity was: _____

_____

The most memorable thing about this trip was: _____

_____

The most fun thing about this trip was: _____

_____

Next time we come back, we must remember to: _____

_____

Our favorite things and places to eat: _____

_____

_____

Other Notes:

A drawing or photo of the favorite part of our stay:

Campground: _____

_____

FROM   TO

Dates: _____   _____

Location: _____

_____ We stayed at site number: _____

Weather: ☀ ☁ ⛅ 🌧 ⛈ 🌬   Score: 1 2 3 4 5 6 7 8 9 10

Who was on this trip with us: _____

_____

_____

Our favorite activity was: _____

_____

_____

The most memorable thing about this trip was: _____

_____

_____

The most fun thing about this trip was: _____

_____

_____

Next time we come back, we must remember to: _____

_____

_____

Our favorite things and places to eat: _____

_____

_____

Other Notes:_____

A drawing or photo of the favorite part of our stay:

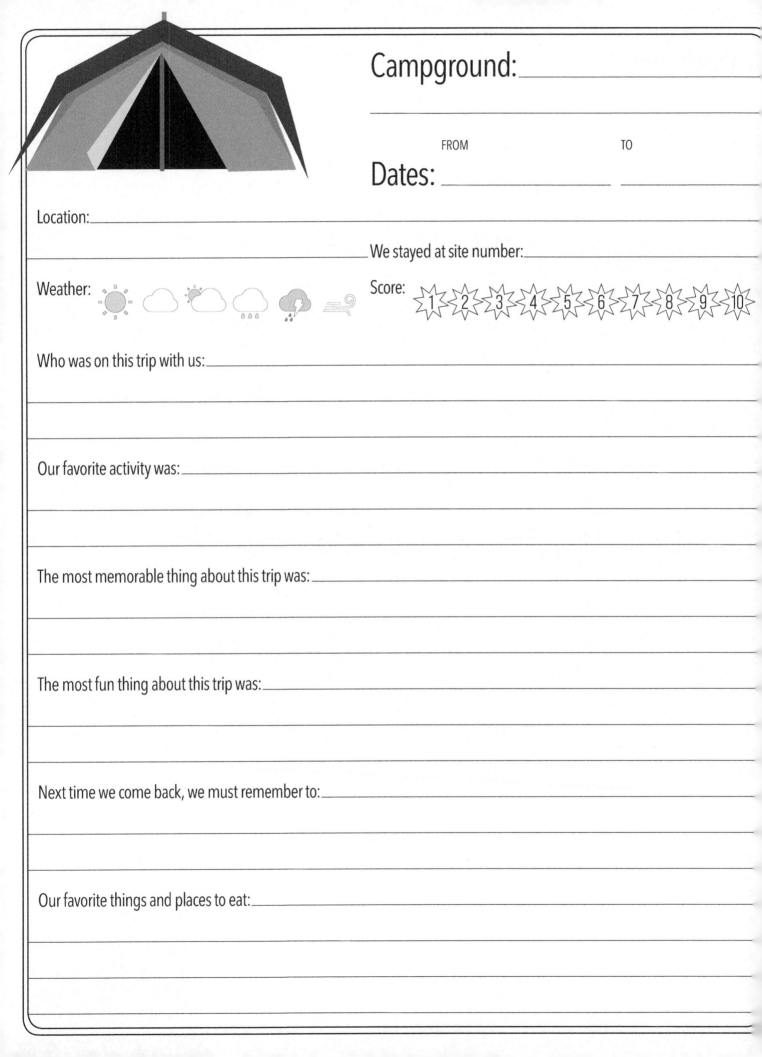

Campground: _____

_____

FROM | TO

Dates: _____ _____

Location: _____

We stayed at site number: _____

Weather: ☀ ☁ ⛅ 🌧 ⛈ 🌬

Score: 1 2 3 4 5 6 7 8 9 10

Who was on this trip with us: _____

Our favorite activity was: _____

The most memorable thing about this trip was: _____

The most fun thing about this trip was: _____

Next time we come back, we must remember to: _____

Our favorite things and places to eat: _____

Other Notes:_____

_____

_____

_____

_____

_____

_____

_____

_____

_____

_____

A drawing or photo of the favorite part of our stay:

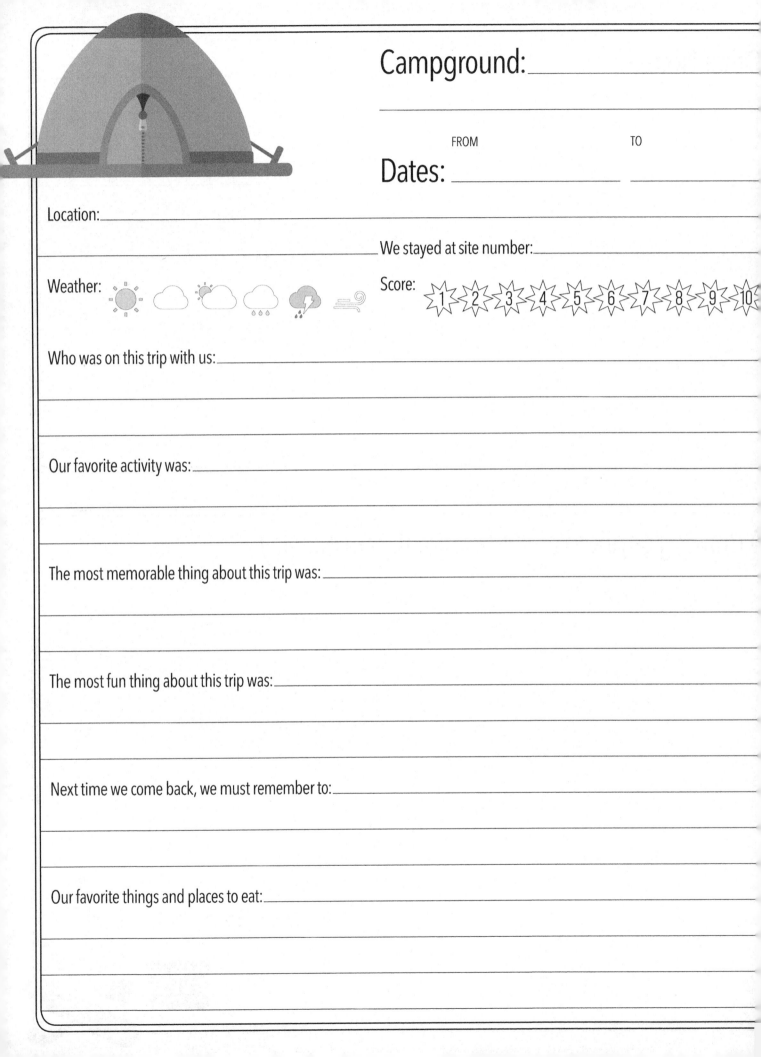

Campground:_____

FROM   TO

Dates: _____   _____

Location:_____

We stayed at site number:_____

Weather:

Score: 1 2 3 4 5 6 7 8 9 10

Who was on this trip with us:_____

Our favorite activity was:_____

The most memorable thing about this trip was:_____

The most fun thing about this trip was:_____

Next time we come back, we must remember to:_____

Our favorite things and places to eat:_____

Other Notes:

A drawing or photo of the favorite part of our stay:

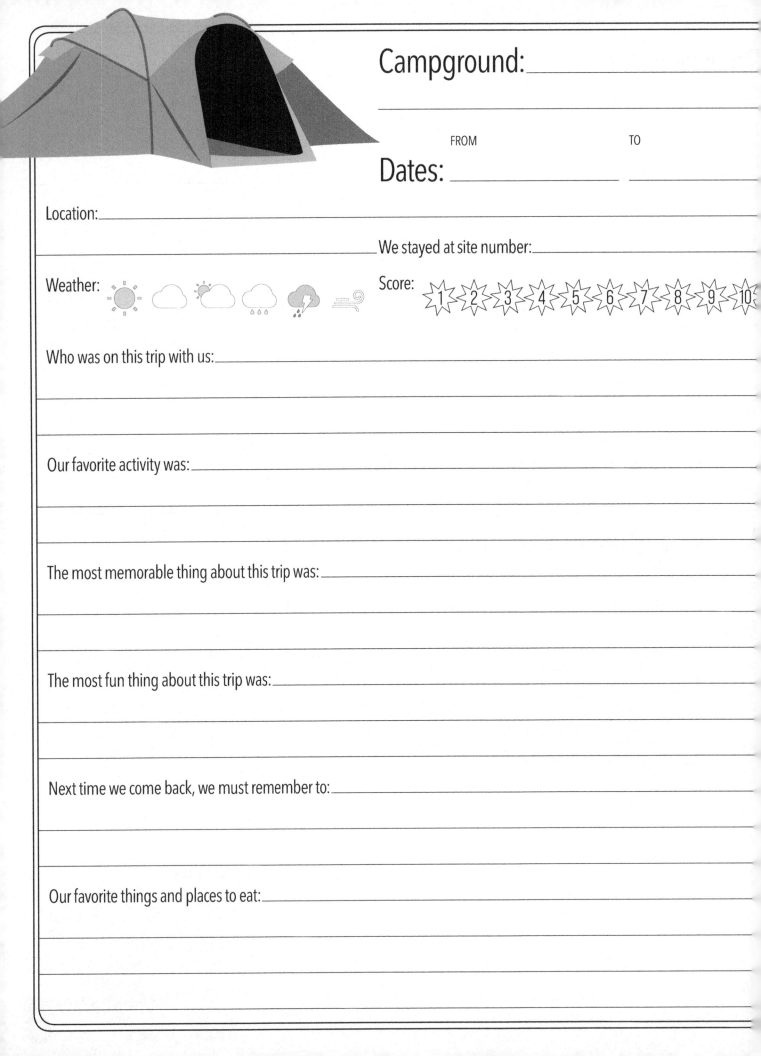

Campground: _____

_____

FROM   TO

Dates: _____   _____

Location: _____

We stayed at site number: _____

Weather: ☀ ☁ ⛅ 🌧 ⛈ 🌬   Score: 1 2 3 4 5 6 7 8 9 10

Who was on this trip with us: _____

_____

_____

Our favorite activity was: _____

_____

_____

The most memorable thing about this trip was: _____

_____

_____

The most fun thing about this trip was: _____

_____

_____

Next time we come back, we must remember to: _____

_____

_____

Our favorite things and places to eat: _____

_____

_____

Other Notes:_____
_____
_____
_____
_____
_____
_____
_____
_____
_____
_____

A drawing or photo of the favorite part of our stay:

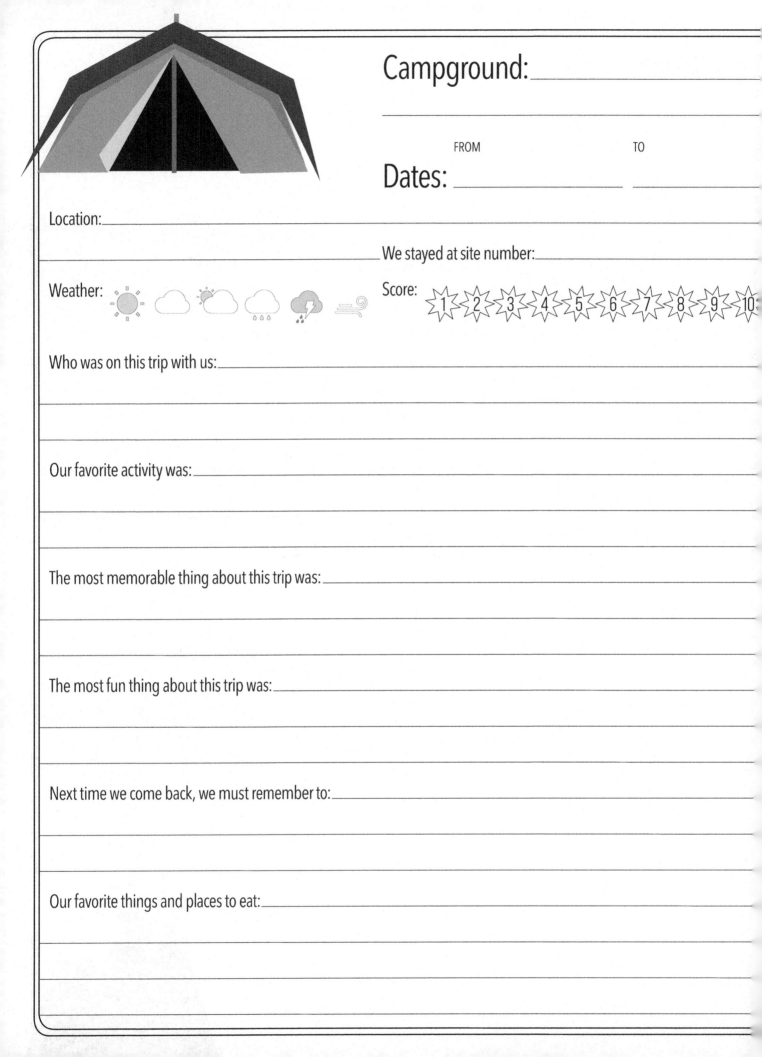

Campground: _____

_____

FROM _____ TO _____

Dates: _____ _____

Location: _____

We stayed at site number: _____

Weather:

Score: 1 2 3 4 5 6 7 8 9 10

Who was on this trip with us: _____

_____

_____

Our favorite activity was: _____

_____

_____

The most memorable thing about this trip was: _____

_____

_____

The most fun thing about this trip was: _____

_____

_____

Next time we come back, we must remember to: _____

_____

_____

Our favorite things and places to eat: _____

_____

_____

Other Notes:

A drawing or photo of the favorite part of our stay:

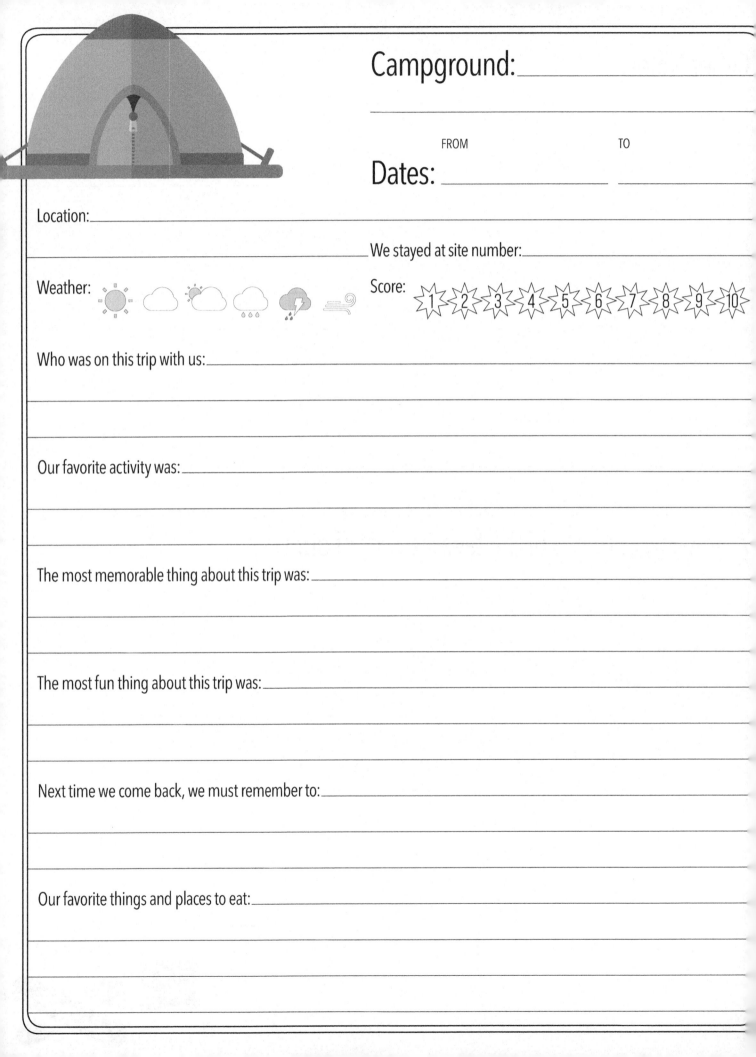

Campground: _____

_____

FROM   TO

Dates: _____   _____

Location: _____

_____ We stayed at site number: _____

Weather: ☀ ☁ ⛅ 🌧 ⛈ 🌬   Score: ✦1 ✦2 ✦3 ✦4 ✦5 ✦6 ✦7 ✦8 ✦9 ✦10

Who was on this trip with us: _____

_____

_____

_____

Our favorite activity was: _____

_____

_____

_____

The most memorable thing about this trip was: _____

_____

_____

_____

The most fun thing about this trip was: _____

_____

_____

_____

Next time we come back, we must remember to: _____

_____

_____

_____

Our favorite things and places to eat: _____

_____

_____

_____

Other Notes:

A drawing or photo of the favorite part of our stay:

Campground: _____

_____

FROM _____ TO _____

Dates: _____

Location: _____

We stayed at site number: _____

Weather: ☀ ☁ ⛅ 🌧 ⛈ 🌬

Score: 1 2 3 4 5 6 7 8 9 10

Who was on this trip with us: _____

_____

Our favorite activity was: _____

_____

The most memorable thing about this trip was: _____

_____

The most fun thing about this trip was: _____

_____

Next time we come back, we must remember to: _____

_____

Our favorite things and places to eat: _____

_____

Other Notes:

A drawing or photo of the favorite part of our stay:

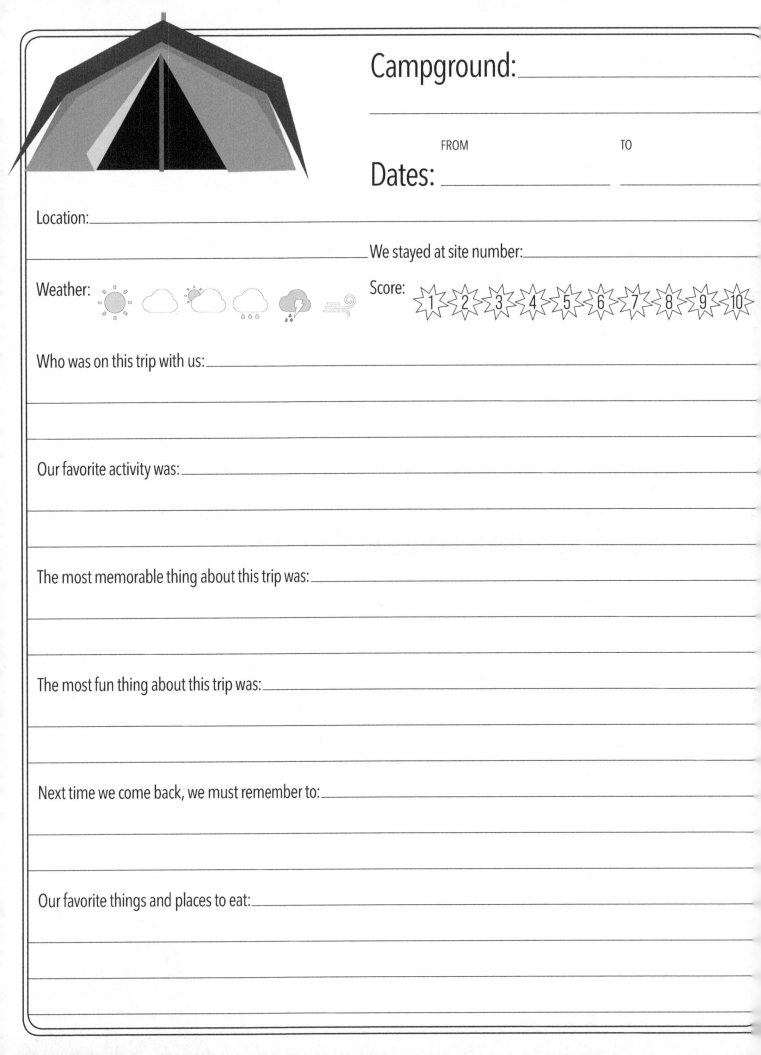

Campground: _____

FROM _____ TO _____
Dates: _____ _____

Location: _____

We stayed at site number: _____

Weather: ☀ ☁ ⛅ 🌧 ⛈ 🌬   Score: 1 2 3 4 5 6 7 8 9 10

Who was on this trip with us: _____

_____

Our favorite activity was: _____

_____

The most memorable thing about this trip was: _____

_____

The most fun thing about this trip was: _____

_____

Next time we come back, we must remember to: _____

_____

Our favorite things and places to eat: _____

_____

Other Notes:_____

_____

_____

_____

_____

_____

_____

_____

_____

_____

_____

_____

A drawing or photo of the favorite part of our stay:

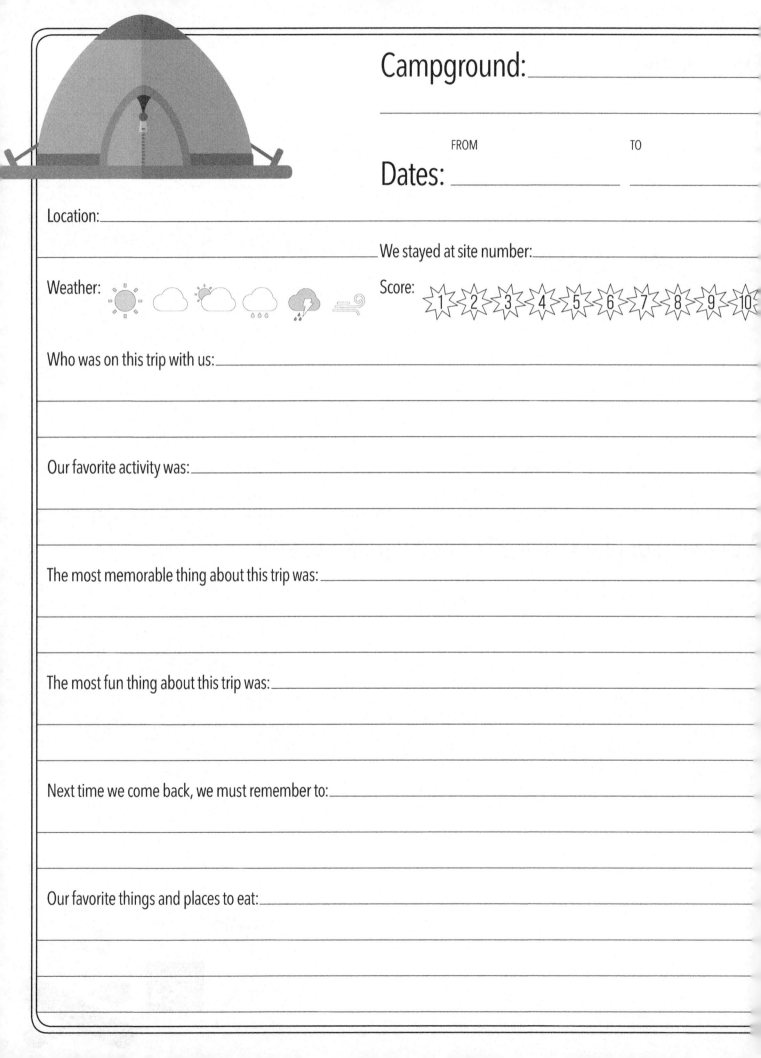

Campground: _____

FROM   TO

Dates: _____   _____

Location: _____

_____ We stayed at site number: _____

Weather: ☀ ☁ ⛅ 🌧 ⛈ 🌬   Score: 1 2 3 4 5 6 7 8 9 10

Who was on this trip with us: _____

_____

_____

_____

Our favorite activity was: _____

_____

_____

_____

The most memorable thing about this trip was: _____

_____

_____

_____

The most fun thing about this trip was: _____

_____

_____

_____

Next time we come back, we must remember to: _____

_____

_____

_____

Our favorite things and places to eat: _____

_____

_____

_____

Other Notes:

A drawing or photo of the favorite part of our stay:

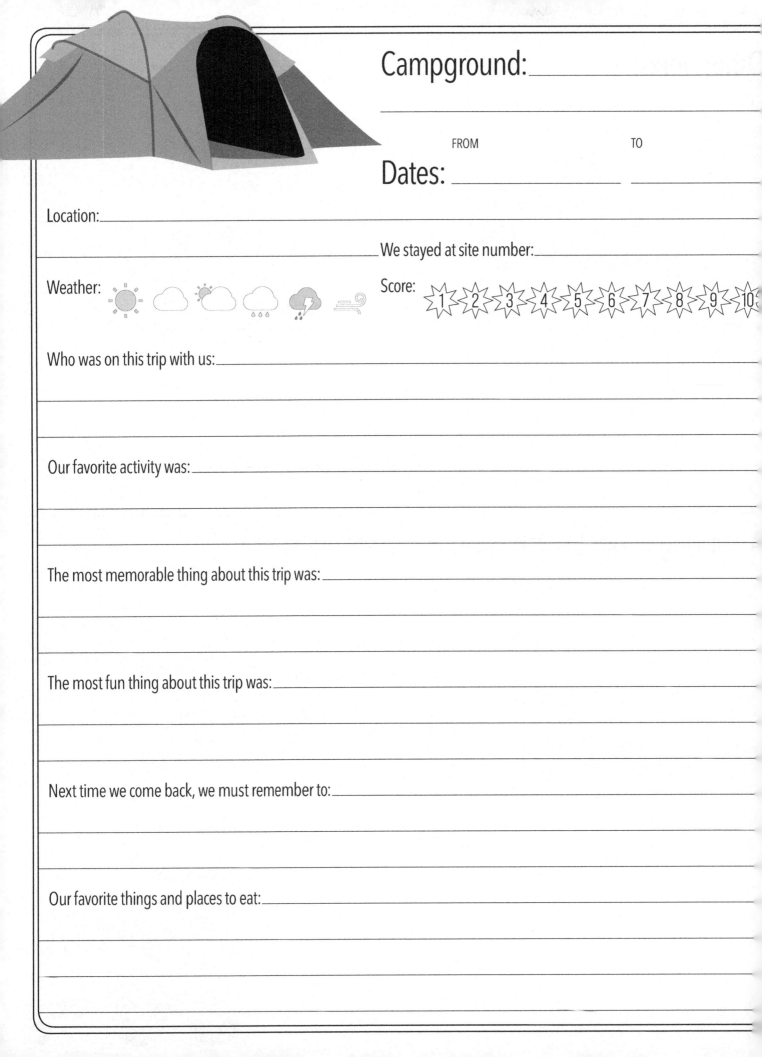

Campground:_____

_____

FROM   TO

Dates: _____ _____

Location:_____

_____ We stayed at site number:_____

Weather: ☀ ☁ ⛅ 🌧 ⛈ 🌬

Score: 1 2 3 4 5 6 7 8 9 10

Who was on this trip with us:_____

_____

_____

Our favorite activity was:_____

_____

_____

The most memorable thing about this trip was:_____

_____

_____

The most fun thing about this trip was:_____

_____

_____

Next time we come back, we must remember to:_____

_____

_____

Our favorite things and places to eat:_____

_____

_____

_____

Other Notes:
_____

A drawing or photo of the favorite part of our stay:

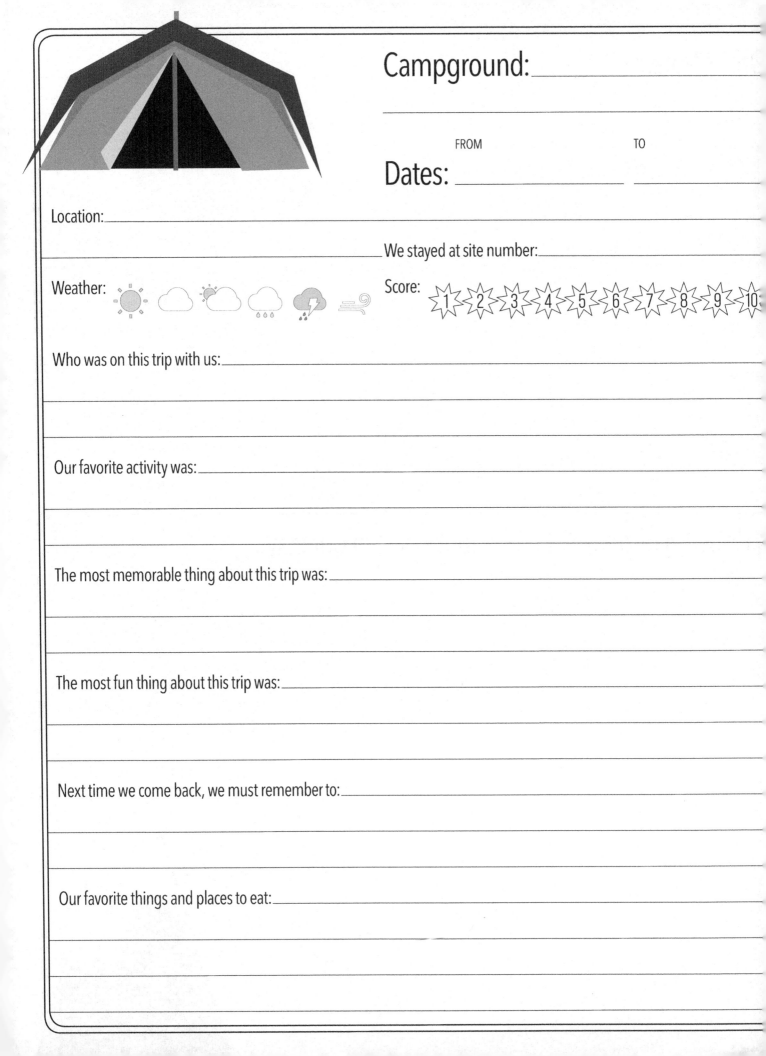

Campground: _____

_____

FROM   TO

Dates: _____   _____

Location: _____

_____

We stayed at site number: _____

Weather: ☀ ☁ ⛅ 🌧 ⛈ 🌬

Score: 1 2 3 4 5 6 7 8 9 10

Who was on this trip with us: _____

_____

_____

Our favorite activity was: _____

_____

_____

The most memorable thing about this trip was: _____

_____

_____

The most fun thing about this trip was: _____

_____

_____

Next time we come back, we must remember to: _____

_____

_____

Our favorite things and places to eat: _____

_____

_____

Other Notes:

A drawing or photo of the favorite part of our stay:

Campground: _____

_____

Dates:

FROM _____ TO _____

Location: _____

_____

We stayed at site number: _____

Weather: ☀ ☁ ⛅ 🌧 ⛈ 🌬

Score: 1 2 3 4 5 6 7 8 9 10

Who was on this trip with us: _____

_____

_____

Our favorite activity was: _____

_____

_____

The most memorable thing about this trip was: _____

_____

_____

The most fun thing about this trip was: _____

_____

_____

Next time we come back, we must remember to: _____

_____

_____

Our favorite things and places to eat: _____

_____

_____

Other Notes:

_____

_____

_____

_____

_____

_____

_____

_____

_____

_____

_____

A drawing or photo of the favorite part of our stay:

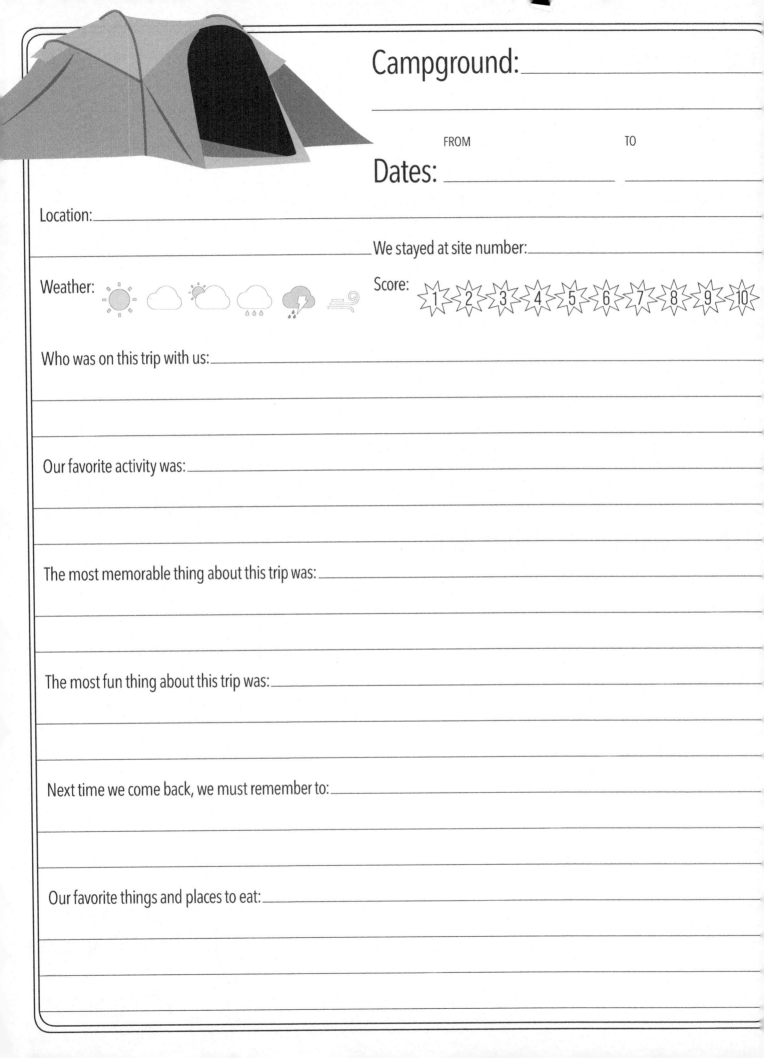

Campground:_____

_____

FROM   TO
Dates: _____   _____

Location:_____

_____ We stayed at site number:_____

Weather: Score: 1 2 3 4 5 6 7 8 9 10

Who was on this trip with us:_____

_____

_____

Our favorite activity was:_____

_____

_____

The most memorable thing about this trip was:_____

_____

_____

The most fun thing about this trip was:_____

_____

_____

Next time we come back, we must remember to:_____

_____

_____

Our favorite things and places to eat:_____

_____

_____

_____

Other Notes:_____

A drawing or photo of the favorite part of our stay:

Campground: _____

_____

FROM _____ TO _____

Dates: _____ _____

Location: _____

_____ We stayed at site number: _____

Weather: ☀ ☁ ⛅ ☁ ⛈ 🌬   Score: 1 2 3 4 5 6 7 8 9 10

Who was on this trip with us: _____

_____

_____

Our favorite activity was: _____

_____

_____

The most memorable thing about this trip was: _____

_____

_____

The most fun thing about this trip was: _____

_____

_____

Next time we come back, we must remember to: _____

_____

_____

Our favorite things and places to eat: _____

_____

_____

_____

Other Notes:

A drawing or photo of the favorite part of our stay:

Campground:_____

_____

FROM   TO

Dates: _____   _____

Location:_____

We stayed at site number:_____

Weather: ☀ ☁ ⛅ 🌧 ⛈ 🌬

Score: 1 2 3 4 5 6 7 8 9 10

Who was on this trip with us:_____

Our favorite activity was:_____

The most memorable thing about this trip was:_____

The most fun thing about this trip was:_____

Next time we come back, we must remember to:_____

Our favorite things and places to eat:_____

Other Notes:
_____

A drawing or photo of the favorite part of our stay:

Campground: _____

_____

FROM _____ TO _____

Dates: _____

Location: _____

_____ We stayed at site number: _____

Weather: Score: 1 2 3 4 5 6 7 8 9 10

Who was on this trip with us: _____

_____

_____

Our favorite activity was: _____

_____

_____

The most memorable thing about this trip was: _____

_____

_____

The most fun thing about this trip was: _____

_____

_____

Next time we come back, we must remember to: _____

_____

_____

Our favorite things and places to eat: _____

_____

_____

_____

Other Notes:

A drawing or photo of the favorite part of our stay:

Campground: _____

_____

FROM   TO

Dates: _____   _____

Location: _____

We stayed at site number: _____

Weather:

Score: 1 2 3 4 5 6 7 8 9 10

Who was on this trip with us: _____

Our favorite activity was: _____

The most memorable thing about this trip was: _____

The most fun thing about this trip was: _____

Next time we come back, we must remember to: _____

Our favorite things and places to eat: _____

Other Notes: _____

A drawing or photo of the favorite part of our stay:

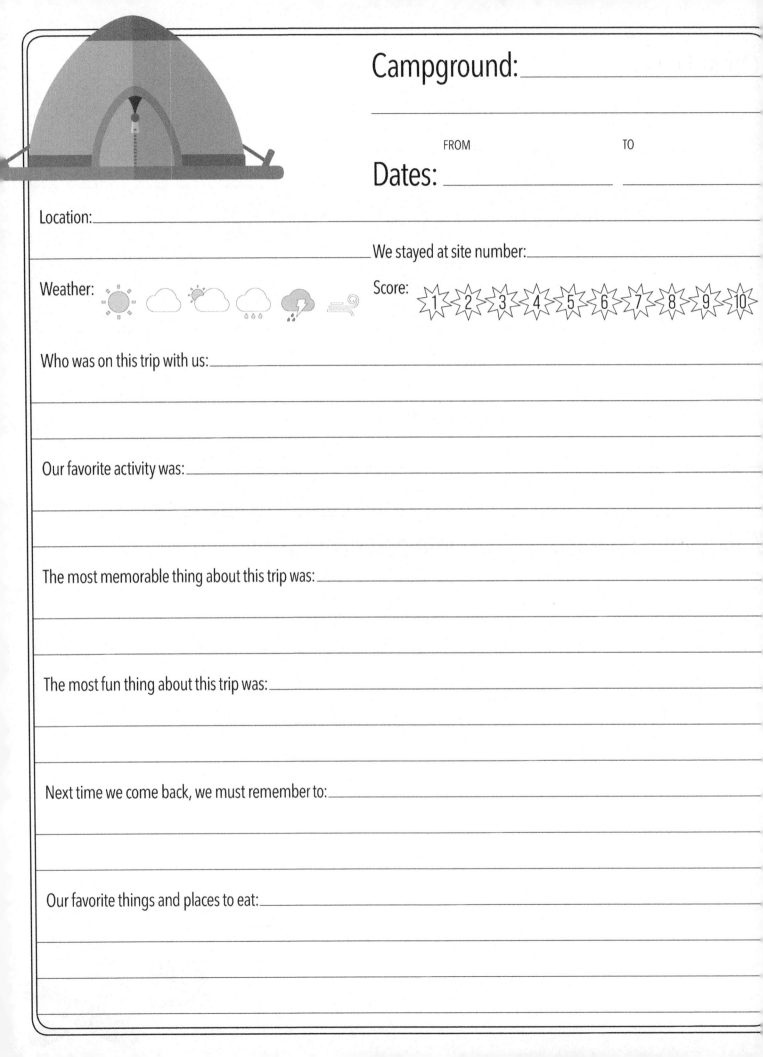

Campground: _____

_____

FROM   TO

Dates: _____   _____

Location: _____

We stayed at site number: _____

Weather:

Score: 1 2 3 4 5 6 7 8 9 10

Who was on this trip with us: _____

_____

_____

Our favorite activity was: _____

_____

_____

The most memorable thing about this trip was: _____

_____

_____

The most fun thing about this trip was: _____

_____

_____

Next time we come back, we must remember to: _____

_____

_____

Our favorite things and places to eat: _____

_____

_____

_____

Other Notes:_____

_____

_____

_____

_____

_____

_____

_____

_____

_____

_____

A drawing or photo of the favorite part of our stay:

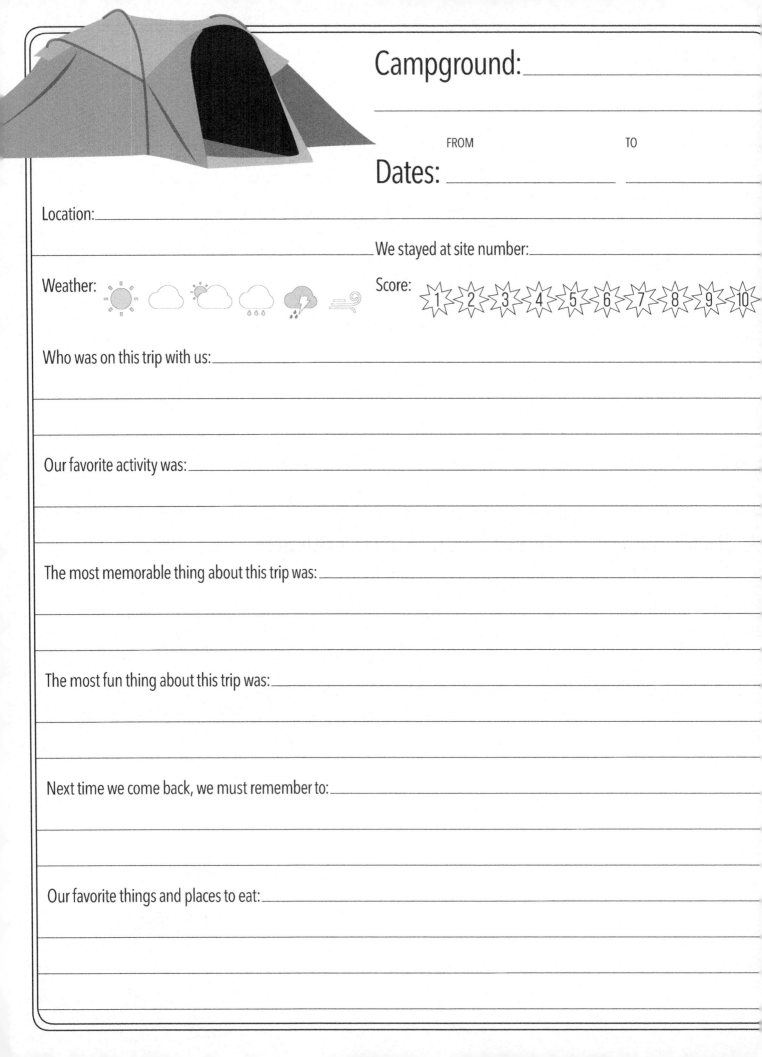

Campground: _____

_____

Dates: _____ _____
FROM   TO

Location: _____

_____ We stayed at site number: _____

Weather: ☀ ☁ ⛅ 🌧 ⛈ 🌬   Score: 1 2 3 4 5 6 7 8 9 10

Who was on this trip with us: _____

_____

_____

Our favorite activity was: _____

_____

_____

The most memorable thing about this trip was: _____

_____

_____

The most fun thing about this trip was: _____

_____

_____

Next time we come back, we must remember to: _____

_____

_____

Our favorite things and places to eat: _____

_____

_____

_____

Other Notes:_____

A drawing or photo of the favorite part of our stay:

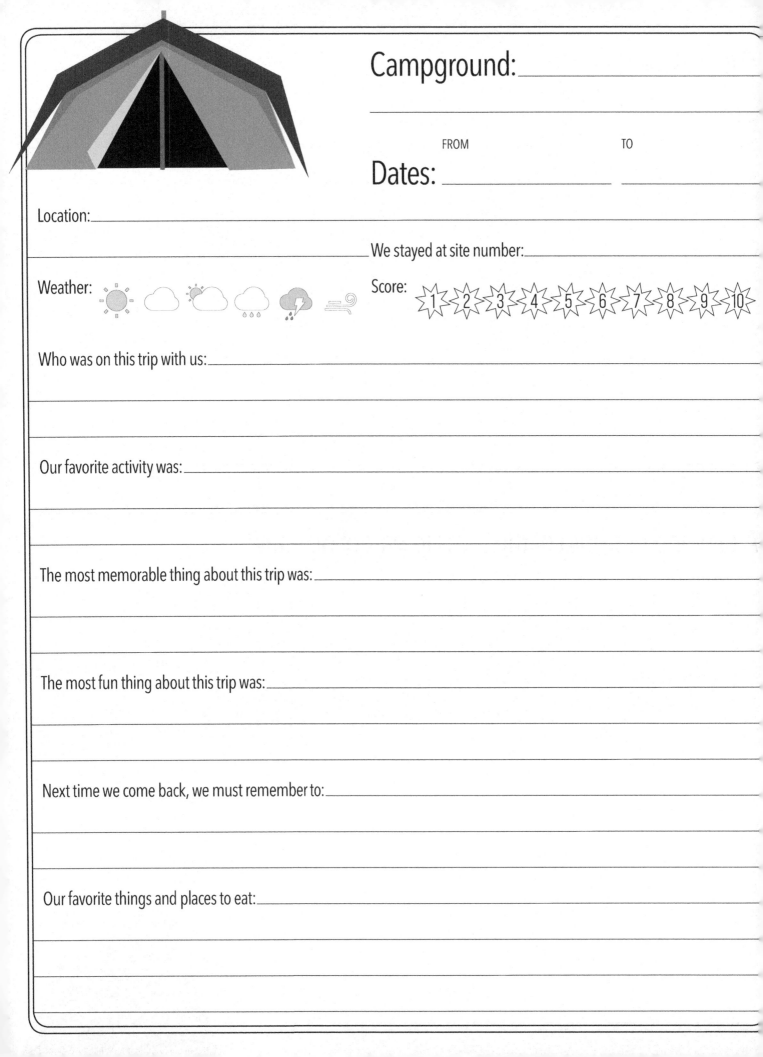

Campground: _____

_____

FROM   TO

Dates: _____   _____

Location: _____

_____

We stayed at site number: _____

Weather: ☀ ☁ ⛅ 🌧 ⛈ 🌬

Score: 1 2 3 4 5 6 7 8 9 10

Who was on this trip with us: _____

_____

_____

Our favorite activity was: _____

_____

_____

The most memorable thing about this trip was: _____

_____

_____

The most fun thing about this trip was: _____

_____

_____

Next time we come back, we must remember to: _____

_____

_____

Our favorite things and places to eat: _____

_____

_____

Other Notes:_____
_____
_____
_____
_____
_____
_____
_____
_____
_____
_____

A drawing or photo of the favorite part of our stay:

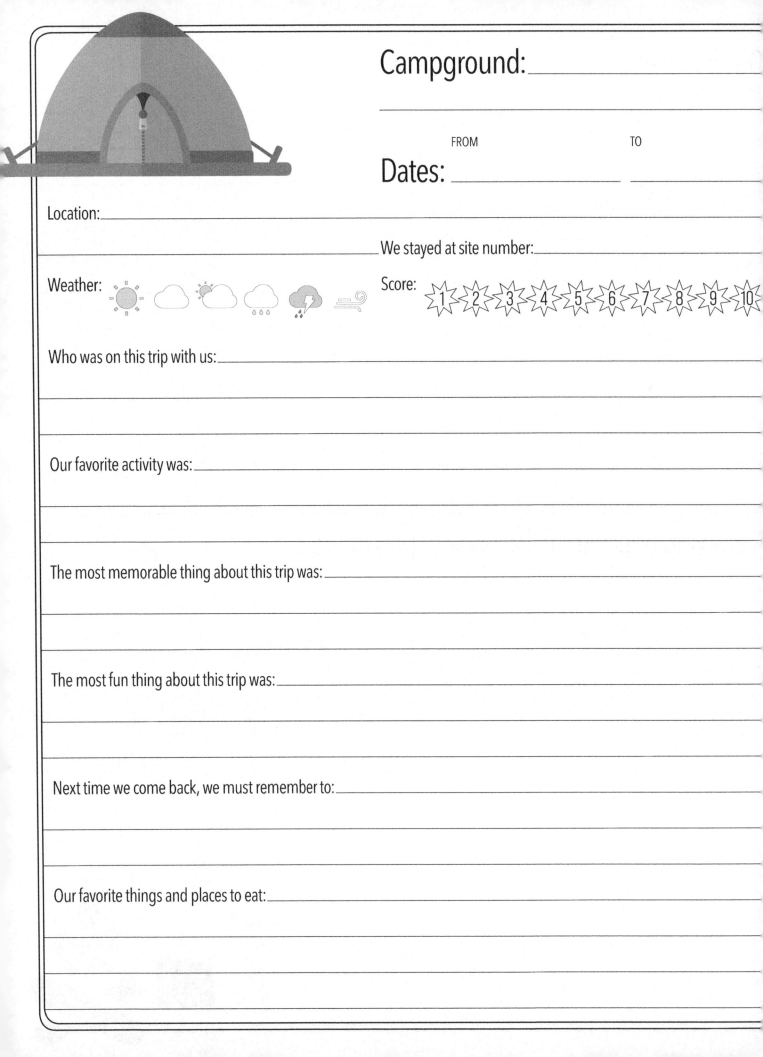

Campground: _____

_____

FROM _____ TO _____

Dates: _____

Location: _____

_____

We stayed at site number: _____

Weather:

Score: 1 2 3 4 5 6 7 8 9 10

Who was on this trip with us: _____

_____

_____

Our favorite activity was: _____

_____

_____

The most memorable thing about this trip was: _____

_____

_____

The most fun thing about this trip was: _____

_____

_____

Next time we come back, we must remember to: _____

_____

_____

Our favorite things and places to eat: _____

_____

_____

Other Notes:

A drawing or photo of the favorite part of our stay:

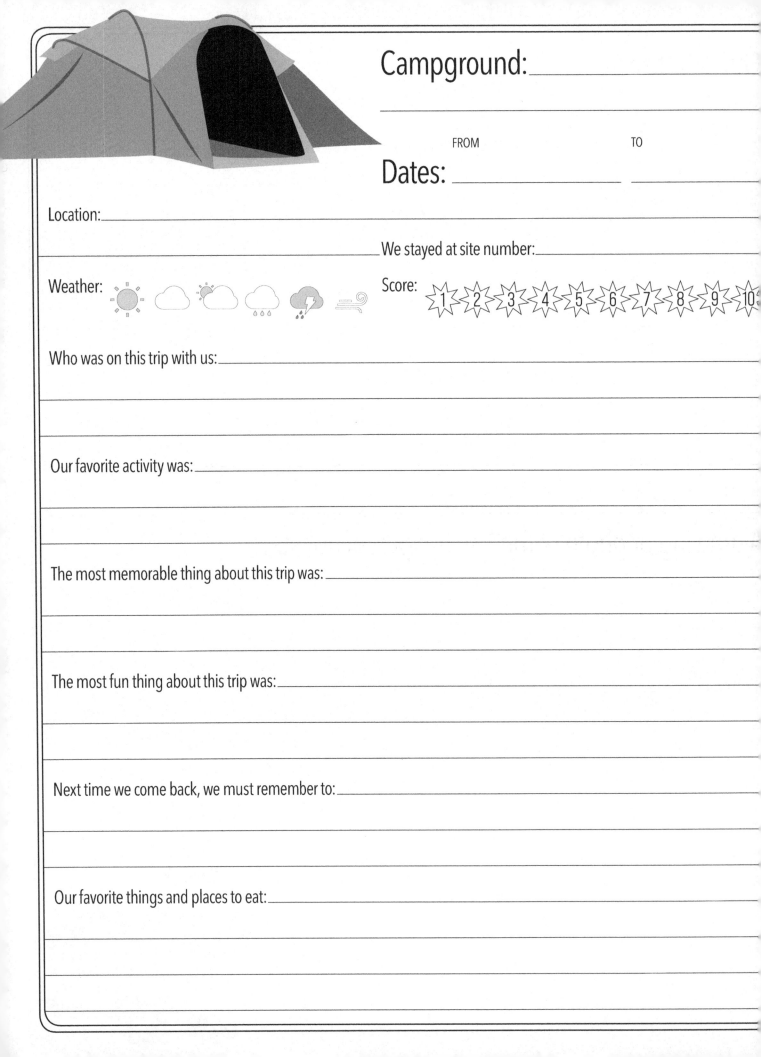

Campground: _____

_____

FROM _____ TO _____

Dates: _____ _____

Location: _____

_____ We stayed at site number: _____

Weather: Score: 1 2 3 4 5 6 7 8 9 10

Who was on this trip with us: _____

_____

_____

Our favorite activity was: _____

_____

_____

The most memorable thing about this trip was: _____

_____

_____

The most fun thing about this trip was: _____

_____

_____

Next time we come back, we must remember to: _____

_____

_____

Our favorite things and places to eat: _____

_____

_____

_____

Other Notes:

_____
_____
_____
_____
_____
_____
_____
_____
_____
_____

A drawing or photo of the favorite part of our stay:

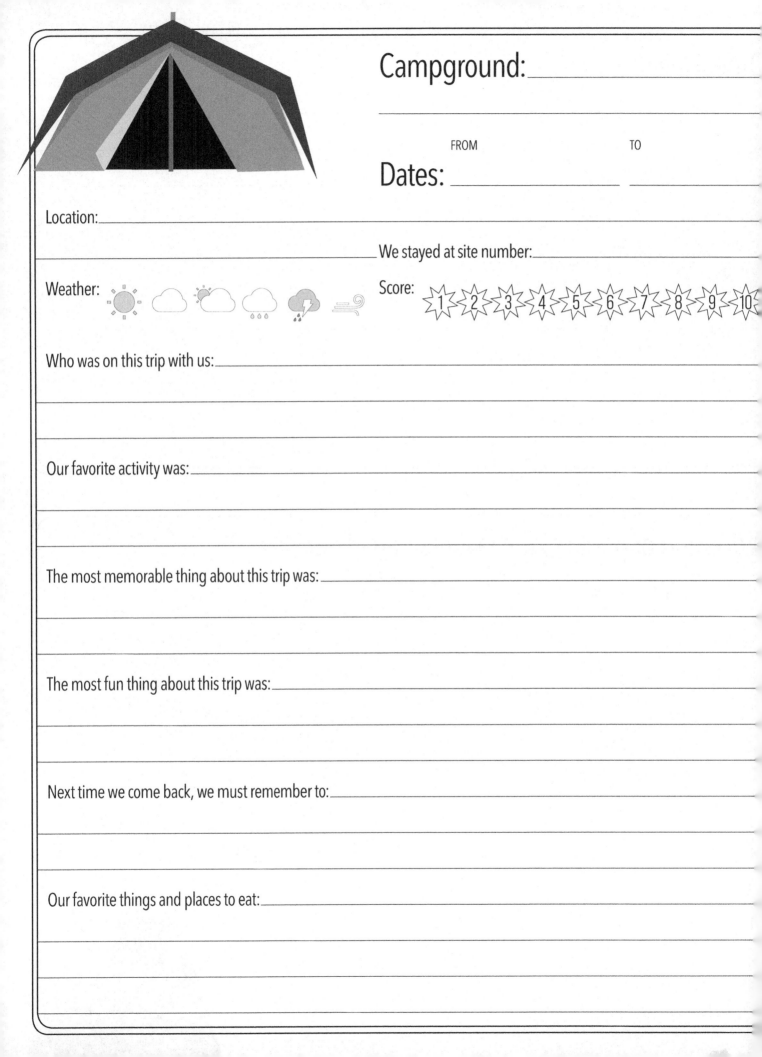

Campground: _____

_____

FROM   TO

Dates: _____   _____

Location: _____

_____

We stayed at site number: _____

Weather: ☀ ☁ ⛅ 🌧 ⛈ 💨

Score: 1 2 3 4 5 6 7 8 9 10

Who was on this trip with us: _____

_____

_____

Our favorite activity was: _____

_____

_____

The most memorable thing about this trip was: _____

_____

_____

The most fun thing about this trip was: _____

_____

_____

Next time we come back, we must remember to: _____

_____

_____

Our favorite things and places to eat: _____

_____

_____

_____

Other Notes: _____

A drawing or photo of the favorite part of our stay:

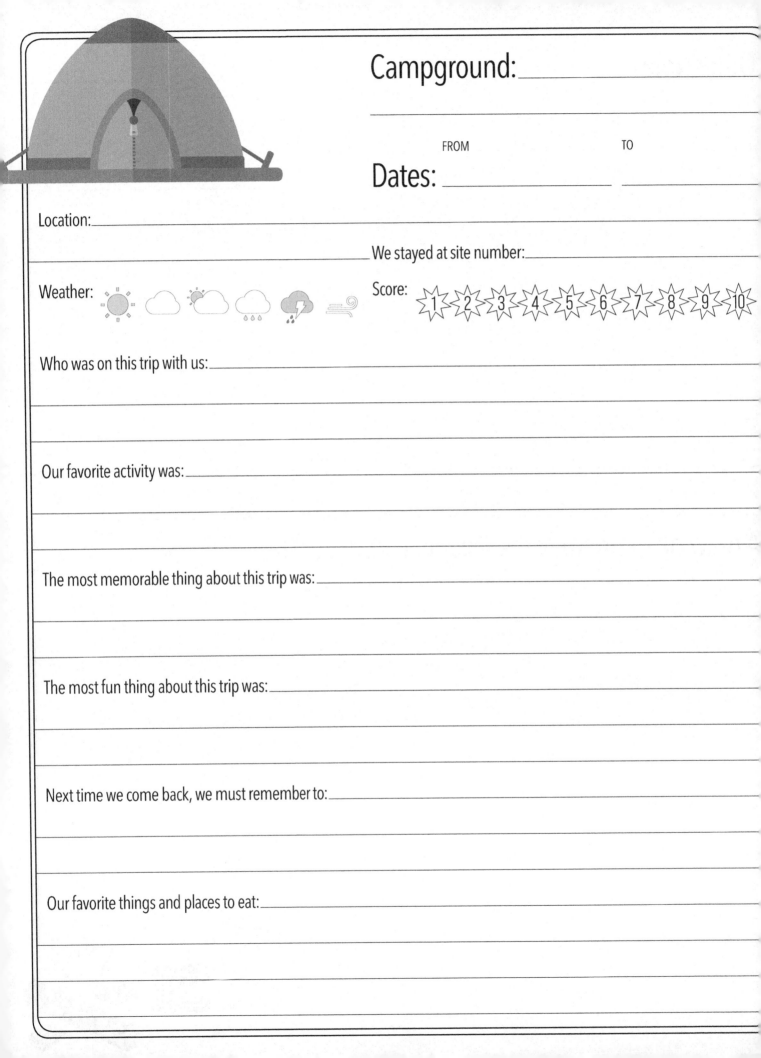

Campground: _____

_____

FROM   TO

Dates: _____   _____

Location: _____

_____ We stayed at site number: _____

Weather: ☀ ☁ ⛅ 🌧 ⛈ 🌬   Score: 1 2 3 4 5 6 7 8 9 10

Who was on this trip with us: _____

_____

_____

Our favorite activity was: _____

_____

_____

The most memorable thing about this trip was: _____

_____

_____

The most fun thing about this trip was: _____

_____

_____

Next time we come back, we must remember to: _____

_____

_____

Our favorite things and places to eat: _____

_____

_____

_____

Other Notes: _____

_____

_____

_____

_____

_____

_____

_____

_____

_____

_____

_____

_____

A drawing or photo of the favorite part of our stay:

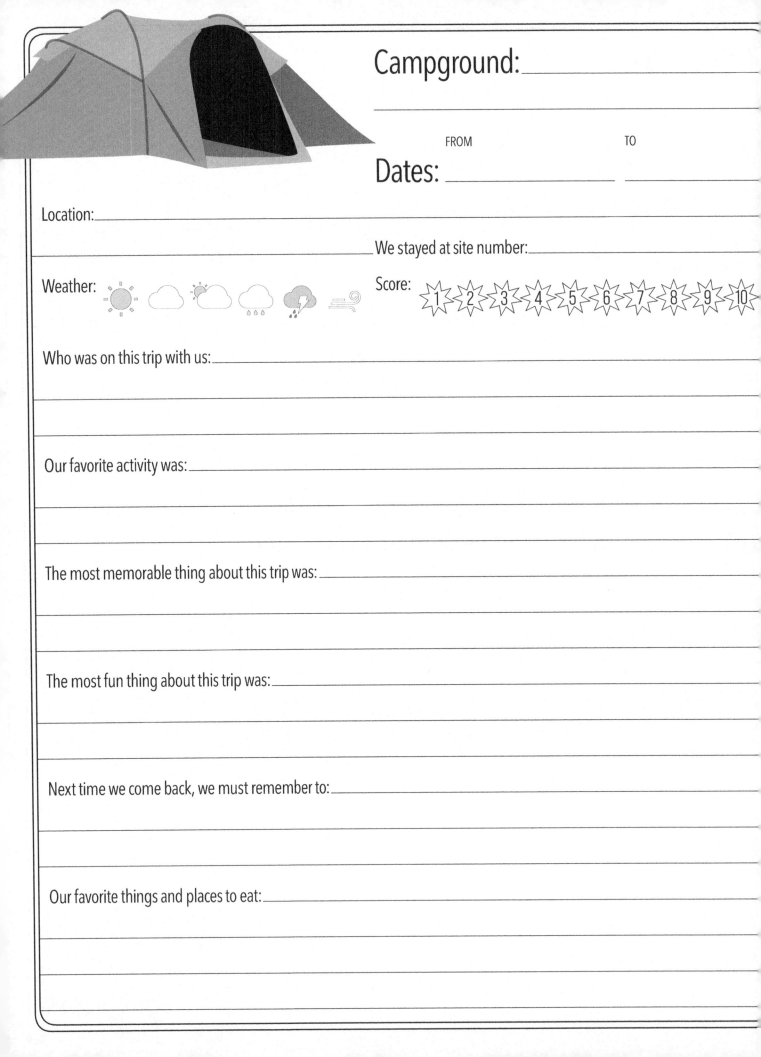

Campground: _____

_____

FROM   TO

Dates: _____ _____

Location: _____

We stayed at site number: _____

Weather: Score: 1 2 3 4 5 6 7 8 9 10

Who was on this trip with us: _____

Our favorite activity was: _____

The most memorable thing about this trip was: _____

The most fun thing about this trip was: _____

Next time we come back, we must remember to: _____

Our favorite things and places to eat: _____

Other Notes:_____

A drawing or photo of the favorite part of our stay:

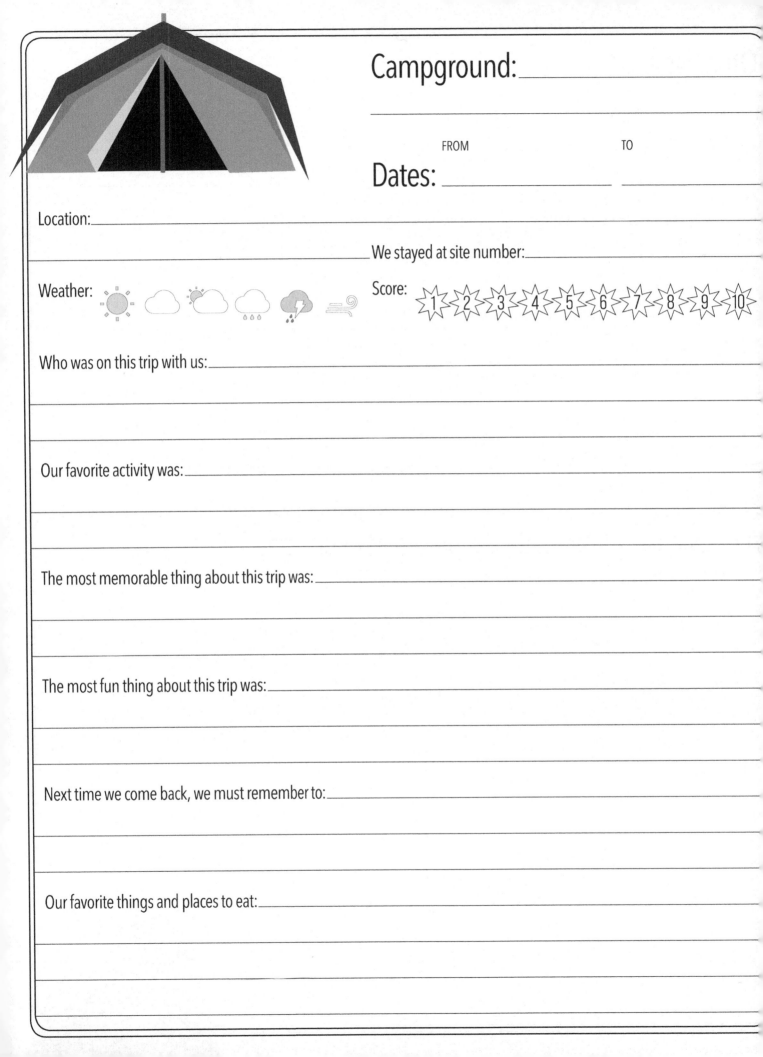

Campground: _____

_____

FROM   TO

Dates: _____ _____

Location: _____

_____ We stayed at site number: _____

Weather: ☀ ☁ ⛅ 🌧 ⛈ 🌬   Score: 1 2 3 4 5 6 7 8 9 10

Who was on this trip with us: _____

_____

Our favorite activity was: _____

_____

_____

The most memorable thing about this trip was: _____

_____

_____

The most fun thing about this trip was: _____

_____

_____

Next time we come back, we must remember to: _____

_____

_____

Our favorite things and places to eat: _____

_____

_____

Other Notes:_____

_____

_____

_____

_____

_____

_____

_____

_____

_____

A drawing or photo of the favorite part of our stay:

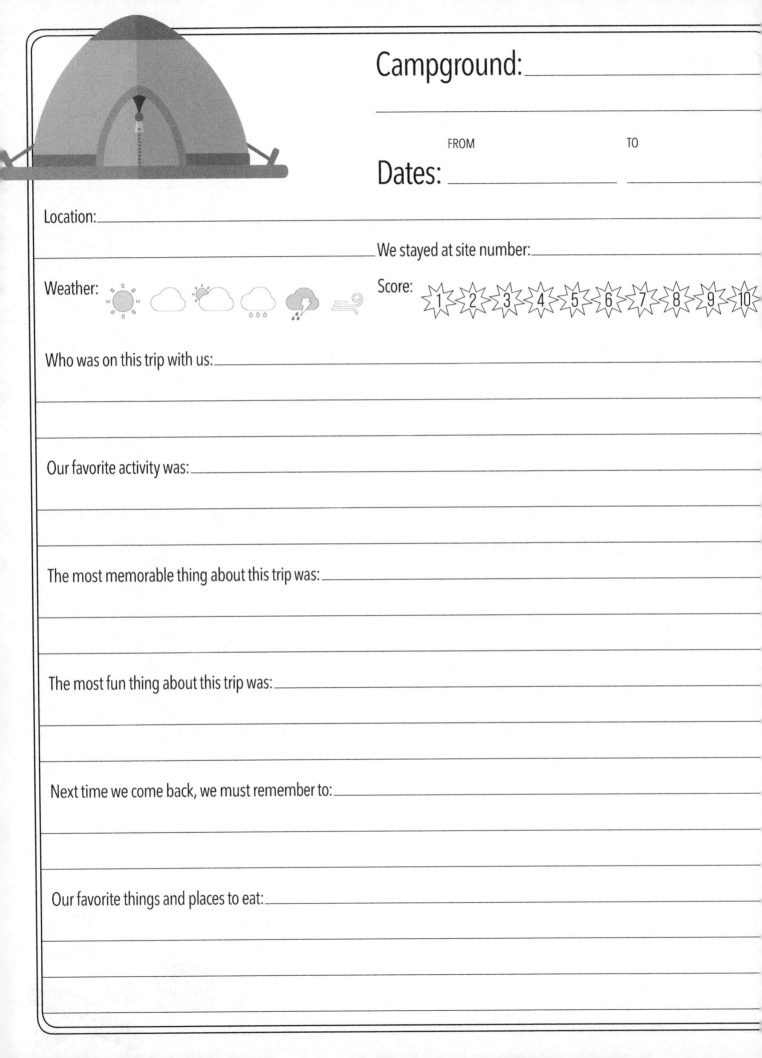

Campground:_____

_____

FROM   TO

Dates: _____   _____

Location:_____

_____ We stayed at site number:_____

Weather: ☀ ☁ ⛅ 🌧 ⛈ 💨   Score: 1 2 3 4 5 6 7 8 9 10

Who was on this trip with us:_____

_____

_____

Our favorite activity was:_____

_____

_____

The most memorable thing about this trip was:_____

_____

_____

The most fun thing about this trip was:_____

_____

_____

Next time we come back, we must remember to:_____

_____

_____

Our favorite things and places to eat:_____

_____

_____

Other Notes:
_____
_____
_____
_____
_____
_____
_____
_____
_____
_____
_____
_____

A drawing or photo of the favorite part of our stay:

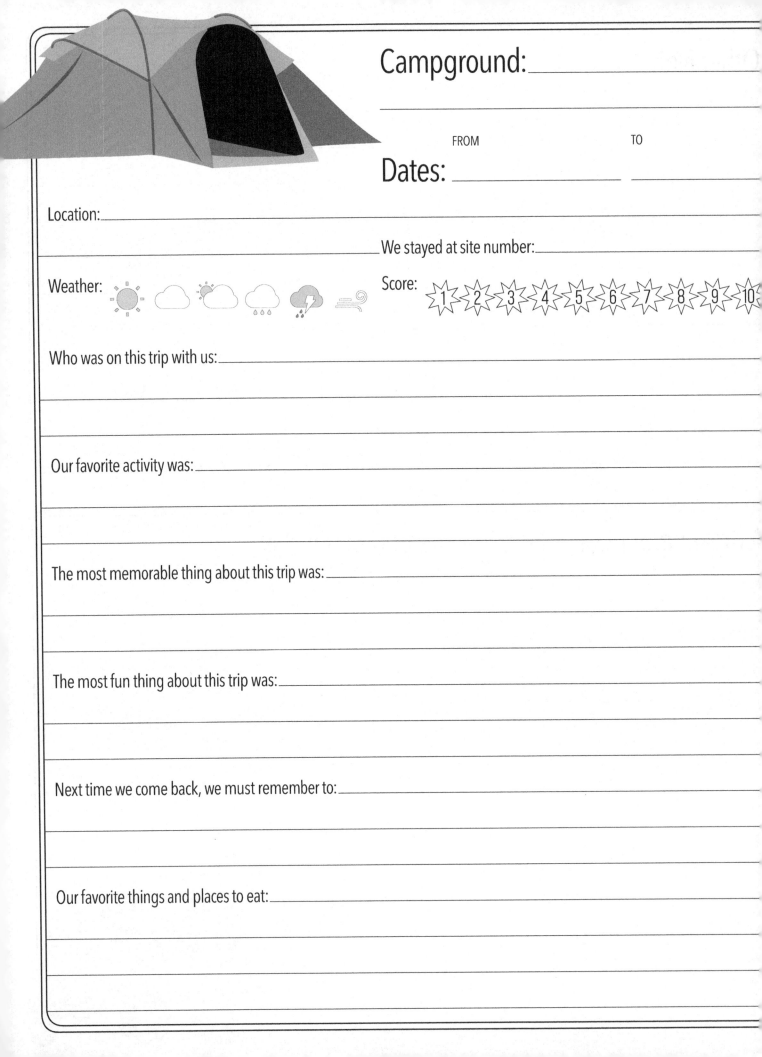

Campground:_____

_____

FROM   TO

Dates: _____ _____

Location:_____

_____ We stayed at site number:_____

Weather: ☀ ☁ ⛅ 🌧 ⛈ 🌬   Score: 1 2 3 4 5 6 7 8 9 10

Who was on this trip with us:_____

_____

_____

Our favorite activity was:_____

_____

_____

The most memorable thing about this trip was:_____

_____

_____

The most fun thing about this trip was:_____

_____

_____

Next time we come back, we must remember to:_____

_____

_____

Our favorite things and places to eat:_____

_____

_____

_____

Other Notes:

_____

_____

_____

_____

_____

_____

_____

_____

_____

_____

_____

_____

A drawing or photo of the favorite part of our stay:

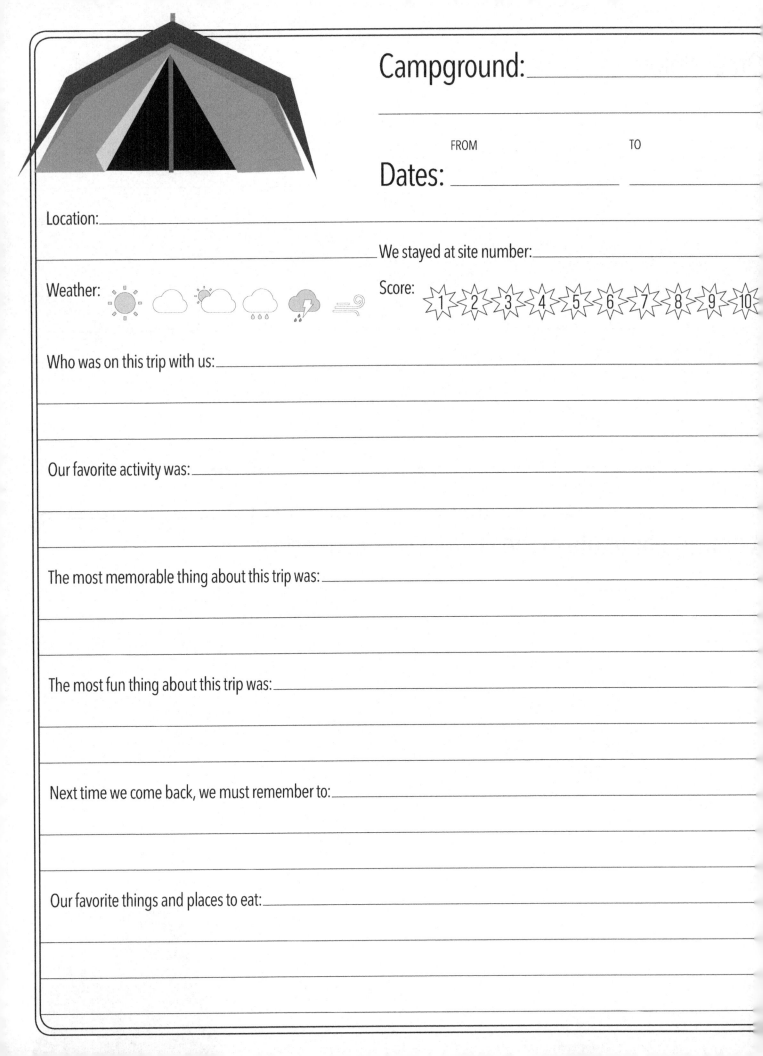

Campground: _____

FROM   TO

Dates: _____   _____

Location: _____

_____ We stayed at site number: _____

Weather: ☀ ☁ ⛅ 🌧 ⛈ 🌬   Score: 1 2 3 4 5 6 7 8 9 10

Who was on this trip with us: _____

_____

_____

Our favorite activity was: _____

_____

_____

The most memorable thing about this trip was: _____

_____

_____

The most fun thing about this trip was: _____

_____

_____

Next time we come back, we must remember to: _____

_____

_____

Our favorite things and places to eat: _____

_____

_____

_____

Other Notes:

A drawing or photo of the favorite part of our stay:

Campground: _____

_____

FROM   TO

Dates: _____   _____

Location: _____

We stayed at site number: _____

Weather: ☀ ☁ ⛅ 🌧 ⛈ 🌬   Score: 1 2 3 4 5 6 7 8 9 10

Who was on this trip with us: _____

_____

Our favorite activity was: _____

_____

_____

The most memorable thing about this trip was: _____

_____

_____

The most fun thing about this trip was: _____

_____

_____

Next time we come back, we must remember to: _____

_____

_____

Our favorite things and places to eat: _____

_____

_____

ther Notes:_____

A drawing or photo of the favorite part of our stay:

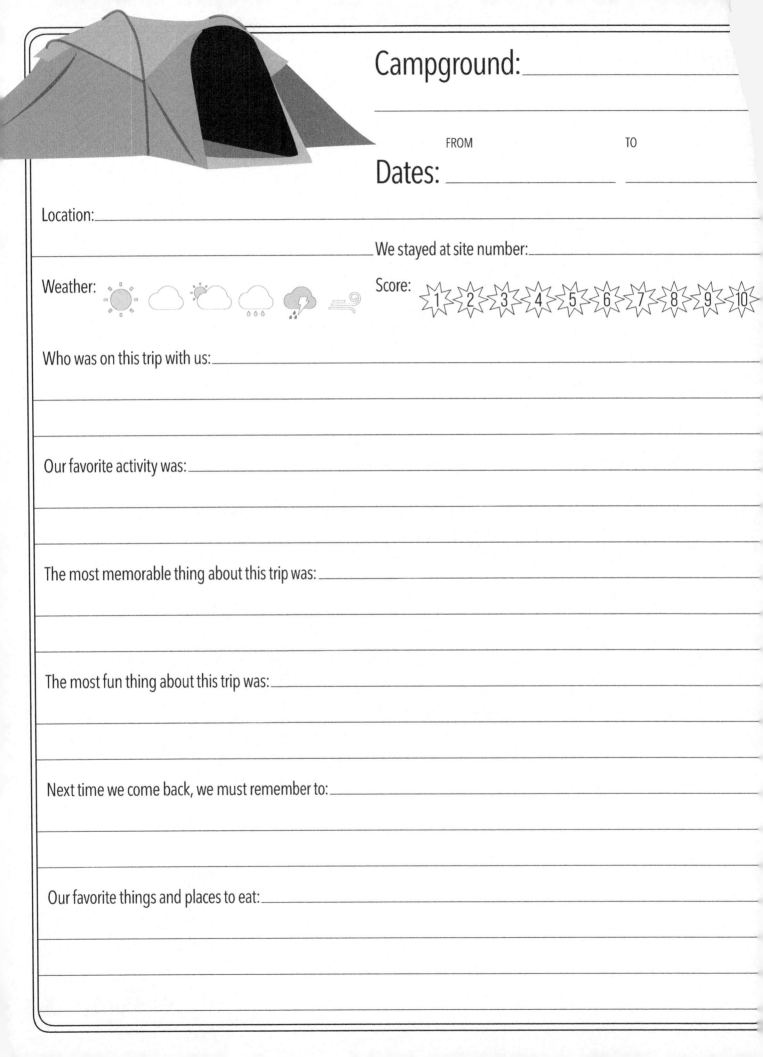

Campground: _____

_____

FROM   TO

Dates: _____   _____

Location: _____

_____ We stayed at site number: _____

Weather: ☀ ☁ ⛅ 🌧 ⛈ 🌬   Score: 1 2 3 4 5 6 7 8 9 10

Who was on this trip with us: _____

_____

_____

Our favorite activity was: _____

_____

_____

The most memorable thing about this trip was: _____

_____

_____

The most fun thing about this trip was: _____

_____

_____

Next time we come back, we must remember to: _____

_____

_____

Our favorite things and places to eat: _____

_____

_____

_____

her Notes:_____

_____

_____

_____

_____

_____

_____

_____

_____

_____

_____

_____

A drawing or photo of the favorite part of our stay:

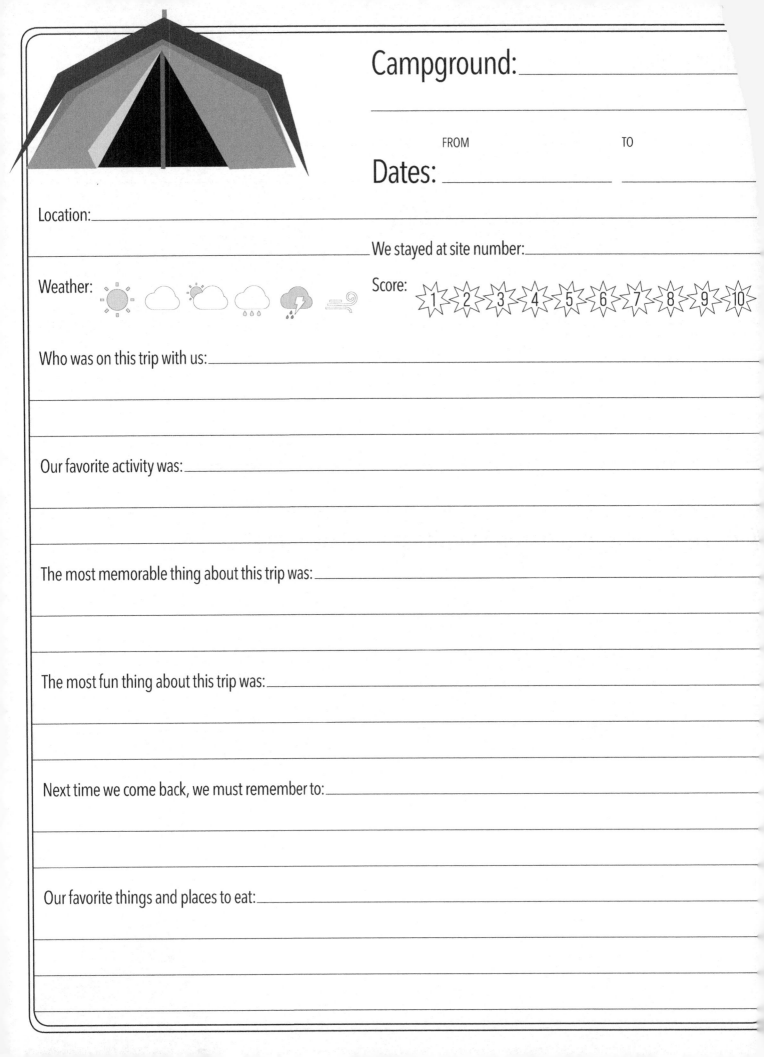

Campground:

Dates: _____ _____
FROM   TO

Location: _____

_____ We stayed at site number: _____

Weather: Score: 1 2 3 4 5 6 7 8 9 10

Who was on this trip with us: _____

_____

_____

Our favorite activity was: _____

_____

_____

The most memorable thing about this trip was: _____

_____

_____

The most fun thing about this trip was: _____

_____

_____

Next time we come back, we must remember to: _____

_____

_____

Our favorite things and places to eat: _____

_____

_____

_____

her Notes:

A drawing or photo of the favorite part of our stay:

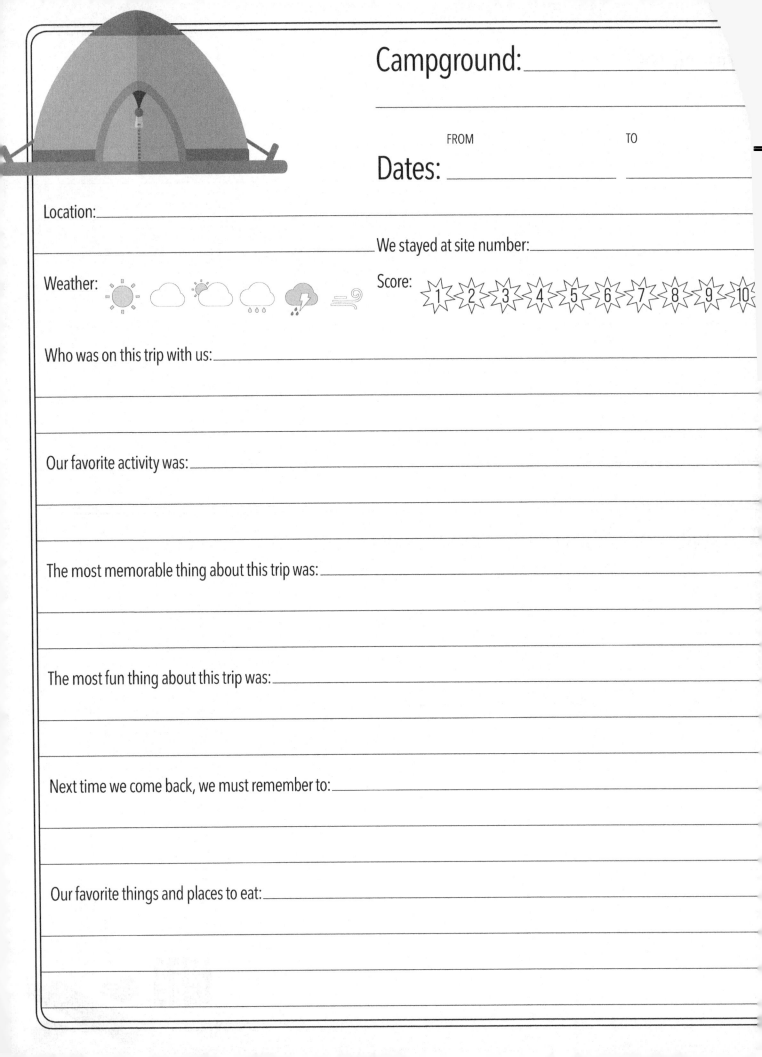

Campground:

FROM _____ TO _____

Dates: _____

Location: _____

We stayed at site number: _____

Weather:

Score: 1 2 3 4 5 6 7 8 9 10

Who was on this trip with us: _____

Our favorite activity was: _____

The most memorable thing about this trip was: _____

The most fun thing about this trip was: _____

Next time we come back, we must remember to: _____

Our favorite things and places to eat: _____

ther Notes:

A drawing or photo of the favorite part of our stay: